Warm and Wet
and other short but occasionally moist plays

Philip Philmar

TSL Drama

First published in Great Britain in 2020
By TSL Publications, Rickmansworth

Copyright © 2020 Philip Philmar

ISBN / 978-1-913294-69-4

Cover art: Phil Davis

The right of Philip Philmar to be identified as the playwright/author of this work has been asserted by the author in accordance with the UK Copyright, Designs and Patents Act 1988.

All characters and events in this publication, other than those clearly in the public domain, are fictitious and any resemblance to actual persons, living or dead, is purely coincidental.

All rights reserved. No part of this publication may be reproduced, stored in a retrieval system or transmitted, in any form or by any means without the prior written permission of the publisher, nor be otherwise circulated in any form of binding or cover other than that in which it is published and without a similar condition being imposed on the subsequent buyer.

Rights of performance

Rights of performance for these scripts is controlled by TSL Publications (tslbooks.uk/Drama) which issues a performing licence on payment of a fee and subject to a number of conditions (specified on tslbooks.uk/Drama). These scripts are fully protected under the Copyright Laws of the British Commonwealth of Nations, the United States of America and all countries of the Berne and Universal Copyright Conventions. All rights, including Online, Stage, Motion Picture, Radio, Television, Public Reading and Translation into Foreign Languages are strictly reserved. It is an infringement of the Copyright to give any performance or public reading of these scripts before the fee has been paid and the licence issued. The Royalty Fee is subject to contract and subject to variation at the sole discretion of TSL Publications. In Territories Overseas the fees quoted may not apply. A fee will be quoted on application to TSL Publications.

Dedication

This book is dedicated to the late John Shaw, a remarkable man who was a brilliant photographer, and creative in many ways; a very important influence in my life—a friend, a supporter and an inspiration, without whom I might not have become a professional actor and writer.

Contents

	Page
Introduction	7
Warm & Wet	9
Fairy-Tale Dress	17
Highly Strung	23
Noah originally titled Waiting For…	29
Police Vet	34
The Wish	41
To Use the Vernacular	48
Death of a Writer	55
Gumpy Forever	62
Stockings, Glimpsed	71
No Business Like It	78
Parts for Males and Females	86
Pause for Thought	98
In, Out, Shake It All About or The 'B' Word	105

Introduction

This is a collection of short, mostly comedy plays I wrote for competitions at "Player Playwrights"—a London based actors and writers' group that provides a critical forum for writing. (For details, search online for the website and Facebook page.)

There are three competitions every year with individual themes, and then a fourth competition—a play-off of all the first and second place winners, to determine which is the best. Most of the plays here came in first or second, and two of the plays included have been judged Best Competition Play of the Year.

The rules were that the play must be longer than 5 minutes and shorter than 10 minutes (a writing discipline challenge), on pain of disqualification. For most of the competitions, a further rule was that there had to be parts for males and females. Each competition consisted of up to 10 plays performed in one evening, script-in-hand with little preparation; so the script had to clearly indicate the writer's intention.

If you are looking for a way to get into script writing, these competitions are great, not to mention fun, and it was how I got started.

These are very short plays indeed. If they were any shorter they probably wouldn't even be plays; yet they are longer, I think, than just sketches, and each one is complete in itself. A number of them might be performed sequentially to create an extended entertainment—a showcase for actors and a set of intriguingly diverse stories for an audience. Certainly they go off in different and I hope unpredictable directions, and it would be challenging to stage them; but with a little imagination, and not being too literal about it, I think perfectly possible. When first performed in competition it was impractical to produce some of the strange props indicated, but the stage directions read aloud was enough to prime the audience's imagination.

A word about swearing: I find the use of indiscriminate bad language, frankly, boring; but there is occasional bad language here, necessary to the characters' ways of expressing themselves. Some of the plays have adult themes.

Warm and Wet

Competition theme: The catch. 2005.
1st place

Set at the British seaside, this would work as a sound only piece—the pictures, as they say, are better on the radio. The scenes are indicated with evocative but simple soundscapes that instantly tell you all you need to know ...

Characters

WILLIAM	40s
GREG	40s
SONARA	(pronounced So-<u>na</u>ra)—female, young but mature and very, very seductive
MAN	20s

Gentle sounds of sea & gulls on a late summer afternoon. Two men sit fishing at the end of an otherwise deserted pier, and one of them lands another fish.

GREG: Up she comes!

WILLIAM: That's your twelfth one!

GREG: Thirteenth, William, thirteenth. [*To the fish*] Gotcha.

WILLIAM: They're not biting for me today. I don't get it, we're using the same bait.

GREG: You haven't got the magic touch, Willie boy.

WILLIAM: What're you going to do with all that fish?

GREG: I'm going to eat it of course!

WILLIAM: You going to eat all that by yourself?

GREG: Yeah. Er, well ... Actually—I'm not that keen on fish, to tell you the truth. I just like catching them. The challenge. Me against them.

WILLIAM: Your grey matter against their fishy matter?

GREG: Exactly. Well, bye.

He gathers his stuff briskly.

WILLIAM: You going?

GREG: [*Leaving*] Yup.

WILLIAM: [*Pause*] Oi, Greg—what are you going to do with all that fish?

GREG: Ahhhm ... chuck it back I suppose.

WILLIAM: Now it's dead?

GREG: Well ... what else am I going to do with it?

WILLIAM: Well I'll have a nice one for my tea if—

Splish, splosh.

GREG: Too late, all gone, you should have said sooner. I'm off. Good luck!

WILLIAM: [*Quietly*] Bastard! Ah, well. Sun's beginning to go down. Perhaps the dead stuff will attract something. I'll just sit here a while more. It's warm and peaceful—who cares if I don't catch anything? [*Yawns*] Tired.

A big splash!

What was that? It was enormous! There's a big one down there somewhere. Or was I imagining it?—Just sunlight on the water. [*Pause*] Nothing now. Been sitting here too long. I'll just pack up and—

Another splash.

There it is again. Bugger me, there is something there, swimming around just below me! Come on boy, this could be it, a really nice catch. Come on, come to me.

SONARA: [*Off*] Hello!
WILLIAM: Oh! What're you doing swimming around at the end of the pier? How long have you been down there?
SONARA: [*Off*] I've been in a while. Come and join me, it's lovely!
WILLIAM: No, I don't swim.
SONARA: [*Off*] Come on I'll teach you.
WILLIAM: Er, no thanks, all the same. [*Beat*] You're ...

She's naked!

SONARA: [*Off*] I'm what?
WILLIAM: You're not wearing a ... you're ... you've not got a—
SONARA: [*Off*] It doesn't matter, there's no one about!
WILLIAM: Well, *I'm* ab ... I suppose not. Well, why not?!
SONARA: [*Off*] Do I embarrass you?
WILLIAM: No, not at all, no, no, I'm very broadminded. Oh yes.
SONARA: [*Off*] The sea caresses you like a lover.
WILLIAM: I dare say.
SONARA: [*Off*] You sure you won't come in with me?
WILLIAM: No thank you. [*To himself*] Oh God if only I could swim!
SONARA: [*Off*] Then, I'll see you on the beach.

WILLIAM: Oh, okay. I'll pack up here and … Oh, she's gone. Right, come on let's get this packed away and oh sod it, I'll get this stuff later!

On the beach, surf and shingle.

WILLIAM: Now where is she? What a tease, I'll bet she's gone and run off already! The sun's really low, almost gone, I can hardly see a thing. Hello? Hello?! Ah well. They'll never believe me in the pub.

SONARA: [*Off*] Hello!

WILLIAM: Hello! Are you coming out? Do you have a towel somewhere? I won't look!

SONARA: I don't mind if you look. I can't come out though. Not without help.

He goes closer.

WILLIAM: Why not? Are you exhausted?

SONARA: No. I don't have any legs!

WILLIAM: You don't have …?

SONARA: Come here.

WILLIAM: Oh!—You don't! You have a … a …

SONARA: Yes.

WILLIAM: You're a—

SONARA: Yes.

WILLIAM: A …

SONARA: Yes!

WILLIAM: A fish.

SONARA: Mermaid!

WILLIAM: Yes. Wow!

SONARA: [*Wiggling provocatively*] Hmm?

WILLIAM: Wow!

SONARA: [*Intimately*] My name's Sonara. What's yours?

WILLIAM: William.

SONARA: Come in with me, William.

WILLIAM:	I can't.
SONARA:	Come.
WILLIAM:	I can't, I told you, I can't swim.
SONARA:	You don't have to, just hold on. Come on—touch me. See—I'm warm.
WILLIAM:	No, I ... Yes you are. You're so smooth, oh, no, my shoes are getting wet.
SONARA:	Take them off, come in!
WILLIAM:	I'd like too. [*Deeper into the surf*] Oh—you won't let me drown?
SONARA:	Of course not. You'll be able to breathe—under water!
WILLIAM:	I'm frightened, oh I'm in up to my waist, no, I'd better not.
SONARA:	Come on, you're in now, hold on to me!
WILLIAM:	Oh, I'm swimming, I'm [*Coughs*] oh, drowning!
SONARA:	Don't be afraid!
WILLIAM:	I'm not, I'm [*Coughs*] I'm drowning, let go, let—
SONARA:	Come on, come down with me, down into the depths, stop struggling, it's just what you deserve.
WILLIAM:	What?
SONARA:	For killing all those fish!
WILLIAM:	What? I didn't!
SONARA:	Murderer!
WILLIAM:	Wha ...?
SONARA:	You murderer, killing all those poor innocent fish!
WILLIAM:	No, no—it wasn't meeeee!

In the pub, chink of glasses, mutter of other drinkers.

GREG:	Yeah, right, you caught a mermaid!
WILLIAM:	Well, she caught me. She nearly had me.
GREG:	She nearly had you.
WILLIAM:	But then I got my hands round her tail—
GREG:	Tail.

WILLIAM:	And I somehow got my feet down into the sand—
GREG:	Sand, yeah, yeah.
WILLIAM:	And I pulled and pulled. She was really strong and I thought I was going to drown a couple of times but I wouldn't let go.
GREG:	You want another drink?
WILLIAM:	And I hauled her up onto the beach and kept on pulling, and she really thrashed about—
GREG:	I'll bet!
WILLIAM:	And we wrestled, and we rolled about ...
GREG:	Nice. [*Beat*] Clean and dry now, though.
WILLIAM:	Went home and changed.
GREG:	Sensible.
WILLIAM:	Oh, she was really furious, thrashing about. But then I ... subdued her.
GREG:	You subdued her.
WILLIAM:	Yeah.
GREG:	Nice tits?
WILLIAM:	I didn't notice.
GREG:	Right. [*Beat*] All right—go on. How did you "subdue" her?
WILLIAM:	Well, I ...
GREG:	Go on.
WILLIAM:	I, er ...
GREG:	Come on—how did you subdue this 'mermaid'?
WILLIAM:	I told her about your prowess with the rod. She's dying to meet you. She's outside. Shall I invite her in? [*Laughs*]

Then both laugh together.

GREG:	All right, I give up, nice one. You got me. What're you having?
WILLIAM:	Same again.

GREG:	Got any cash, I'm all out.
WILLIAM:	Oh, here, take it out of this.
GREG:	[*Off, to the barman*] There you go—keep the change.
WILLIAM:	No. I'll tell you. I did catch one though. Bigger than any you caught.
GREG:	Well, we'll never know will we? Here's your drink.
WILLIAM:	It's in the car. Thanks.
GREG:	Eh?
WILLIAM:	Cheers. I don't throw them back like you do.
GREG:	You got it in the car?
WILLIAM:	Yup.
GREG:	Bigger than any I caught?
WILLIAM:	Yup.
GREG:	Well let's have a look!
WILLIAM:	I'm having my drink now.
GREG:	It'll keep.
WILLIAM:	Well, all right, follow me.
GREG:	Right then.

Car park. Feet on gravel. Bleep of remote unlocking, tailgate opening.

WILLIAM:	[*Scrabbling*] Where are we? Under this tarp somewhere …
GREG:	Come on then, get it out, let's have a look at your …
SONARA:	[*Pause, then, seductively*] Hello Greg.
GREG:	[*Weakly*] Fish.

Another day at the end of the pier.

MAN:	All right mate?
WILLIAM:	Hmm?
MAN:	Mind if I set up here?
WILLIAM:	No, you go ahead.
MAN:	What's the fishing like here? Any idea?

WILLIAM:	Depends what you want to catch.
MAN:	Let's give it a go shall we? D'you fish?
WILLIAM:	Not any more, no.
MAN:	No?
WILLIAM:	Not since the ... accident.
MAN:	Oh? What happened?
WILLIAM:	Man I knew, keen fisherman, got dragged out to sea.
MAN:	No?! Drowned?
WILLIAM:	Probably. Never saw him again.
MAN:	Blimey. Must'a been a big one!—To pull him out to sea!
WILLIAM:	Yeah. Yeah, big. [*Pause*] But beautiful.

THE END

Fairy-Tale Dress

Competition theme: Articles for sale. 1998.
2nd place

My first play for Player Playwrights. At the time, the honorary President of Player Playwrights was the marvellous writer Jack Rosenthal, who would present the prizes. I came 2nd. When Mr Rosenthal presented me with my certificate, he said to me, "I thought it should have done better." I was more delighted with his comment than if I had actually come 1st.

(My girlfriend at the time, the late Lin Rose, gave me some good feedback as I was writing this.)

Characters

HIL	Hilary, 26, to be married very soon
DAD	father of Hilary
WOMAN	middle-aged, with a surprising history

The cosy front room of a suburban semi, sometime pre-Internet. Hilary is with her dad who is reading the small ads in the local paper.

HIL: Remy's mum knows a good cheap caterer, but—oh dad, I know I'm only going to wear it once, but the dresses in our price range at Finches, they were just so tacky—all that nasty nylon. And so shoddy ...

DAD: Here you are Hil, love.

HIL: Hm?

DAD: "Wedding Dress for sale, only worn twice".

HIL: Let's have a look. [*Pause*] I don't know—I don't fancy wearing someone else's cast-offs. Worn twice before ... twice!

DAD: Well it wouldn't hurt to have a look—And you never know, you could save us a fortune.

HIL: What's the number?

***

Hilary and a woman are in a bedroom in an upstairs flat in front of a cheap melamine wardrobe, on which is hanging a fabulous classic white fairy-tale wedding dress.

WOMAN: There—what do you think?

HIL: Oh—it's lovely ... May I try it on?

WOMAN: Of course—shall I help you on with it?

HIL: Oh, please.

> *She takes off her sweater and slips out of her jeans while the woman takes down the dress and unfastens it at the back. Hilary grabs it getting ready to step in. There's a ripping noise.*

HIL: Oh, oh my God—I think I've torn it!

WOMAN: Let me have it a moment—no dear—the sleeve's meant to come off—you see?—Velcro!

HIL: Oh.

WOMAN:	The bodice too. And the petticoats are all separate.
HIL:	That's ingenious—I suppose it makes it easier to put on?
WOMAN:	Well, easier to get off actually ...
HIL:	Oh ...
WOMAN:	It's specially made you see. To my own design. The thing to do is to put it together perfectly, on the hanger, and then carefully put it on—it's quite secure. Then if you want to get it off, in a hurry—you can pull it off, a bit at a time.
HIL:	Y-yes ... Sorry, why would I want to take it off in a hurry?—Oh you mean ... no, I don't know what you mean.
WOMAN:	Well now, I suppose I'd better explain ... you see, when I had the dress made, I had no intention of getting married.
HIL:	Oh.
WOMAN:	It was for ... dressing up.
HIL:	Oh.
WOMAN:	As a bride.
HIL:	Ah.
WOMAN:	And then, undressing. [*Pause*] You see, I used to be a ... dancer.
HIL:	Oh.
WOMAN:	Oh yes—I had some gorgeous costumes—all gone now. I designed them all. Oh yes—they were wild! Satins and feathers and flounces—outrageous! Hmm ...
HIL:	Oh. [*Dawning*] Oh I see, you were a stripper! Oo—sorry!
WOMAN:	No, no you're quite right! I was. But, you know, a classy one—none of that sleazy pub bump and grind.
HIL:	No. No.
WOMAN:	No. And I only wore it the once in my act, dear, but now you know why it was made, I expect you're not interested any more ...

HIL:	Well, it is lovely—and you can't tell it was for a stri ... er, a show. And, I'm going to put it on, if that's still all right.

The woman helps to dress her, then stands her in front of a full length mirror.

HIL:	Oh it looks lovely on ...
WOMAN:	A perfect fit! I knew it would be when I saw you at the door. We have the same figure—had I should say, I'm a little ...
HIL:	Oh it's fabulous—and the price is really reasonable, I could never afford anything like this new ... Remy will really love ... Why did you only wear it once in the show? Your advert said it had been worn twice.
WOMAN:	Yes ... well just after I'd done the new act for the first time, I had to go in to hospital for a while ...
HIL:	Oh, you were ill?
WOMAN:	No.
HIL:	Oh—an accident.
WOMAN:	... No.
HIL:	Oh, I'm sorry, it's none of my business ...
WOMAN:	I had an operation—well, a series of operations you see ...
HIL:	No, I don't, not if you weren't ill—oh, I see—[*lowers her voice*] cosmetic surgery, was it?
WOMAN:	No dear. I had a sex change ... A gender reassignment they called it ... Oh dear, I always thought that sounded like an episode of Star Trek: To boldly go and get a gender reassignment ... Ah well, I can see I have shocked you now. Just slip the dress off and we'll say no more about it. I always tell people more than they want to know.
HIL:	No, look, really that's fine. I mean you're entitled to ... I mean I'm very broad minded. The dress is the important thing and it fits perfectly, doesn't it? Yes ...
WOMAN:	Oh, I'm so glad you feel that way, it deserves to be worn. Some people ...

HIL:	Well, I ... [*Pause*] Er, wait a minute ... Really, I'm OK about this but, if you had a ... an operation, then you were a, you were a man when—[*She indicates the dress*]
WOMAN:	Yes, but I was a woman when I wore it the second time. To get married in!
HIL:	Er ...
WOMAN:	Yes. You see: the first time I wore it I came on as a woman, do you see? but then I gradually reveal that really, underneath it all, I'm a man—stark naked! Ah, but the lighting—very tasteful. But you see, I wasn't.
HIL:	No. What?
WOMAN:	I wasn't a man.
HIL:	But—
WOMAN:	I was, but I wasn't. Inside. I'd been living a lie. So I had the op. Well it didn't happen just like that.
HIL:	No.
WOMAN:	No, it takes years of counselling and therapy. Well you can imagine! But it was the dress that brought me to the point of realisation.
HIL:	And then you got married.
WOMAN:	Well, a little later on ...
HIL:	To a man?
WOMAN:	Of course to a man—I'm not a lesbian!
HIL:	Sorry, I ...
WOMAN:	No dear, you weren't to know ...
HIL:	So then you got married. [*Long pause*] Ah, that's wonderful, that means it is a proper wedding dress after all!
WOMAN:	Yes, there you are!
HIL:	Ah. So where's your husband now? Oh that's none of my business I keep asking embarrassing questions don't I?
WOMAN:	No, you're not embarrassing me.
HIL:	No—I'm embarrassing myself.

WOMAN:	He left me.
HIL:	I'm so sorry.
WOMAN:	Well, it was my own fault. I should have noticed sooner ...
HIL:	He'd been having an affair?
WOMAN:	No dear—he'd been dressing up in all my clothes.

***

Back at home.

DAD:	So, come and tell me all about it. How was the dress?
HIL:	Oh, it was stunning, just stunning ...
DAD:	But?
HIL:	Well, I thought that Remy wouldn't like it, but then I thought he would. But then I thought, well it's me that's got to wear it, isn't it?
DAD:	Exactly, love.
HIL:	And I thought you wouldn't like it.
DAD:	Oh don't you worry about me love, it's you who's got to wear it.
HIL:	Well, perhaps it was too glamorous and I couldn't do it justice.
DAD:	Nonsense—you're as beautiful as your mother was. Sounds like you should have got that dress.
HIL:	It was amazing, but in the end I thought, well—it's just not ... us.
DAD:	[*Pause*] Oh well, never mind, you'll find something.
HIL:	You know what? I'm going to get myself a posh frock instead—yes, something comfortable that suits *me*. And something I can wear more than just once—or twice.

THE END

Competition theme: Anyone for tennis? 1998.
1st place.

Were there ever plays with a young man bouncing in through the French windows declaring the clichéd words of this competition's theme? If so, I don't think they ever played out in quite the same way ... A big country house in the 1920s, two "gay" young things, a butler, a murder mystery and a good deal of silliness. Conceived for sound; I think the jokes work better in this case, when the audience can only hear what's happening.

Characters

EDGAR	a chap
POOKIE	a gel
JEFFERS	a man, quite an elderly butler

England: a big house in the country in the 1920s. As the play starts, Edgar is capering in the garden.

SFX Jolly English summer birdsong.

EDGAR: Hoorah—a perfect day for it! [*Takes a deep appreciative breath*] Where is everyone?

SFX Crunch of feet on gravel, patio door opening into house.

EDGAR: Yoo-hoo! Anyone for tennis?

Pookie is sobbing.

EDGAR: Pookie?
POOKIE: Not just now, Edgar—I simply couldn't!
EDGAR: Oh I say, old thing, why ever not?
POOKIE: Well, look!
EDGAR: [*Beat*] Look at what, old thingy?
POOKIE: A body.
EDGAR: Body? Where?
POOKIE: There. [*Beat—he still hasn't seen it—then all in one breath*] On the rug in front of the fireplace beside the settee between the Aspidistra and the writing desk next to the umbrella stand. [*No, still hasn't seen it!*] On the floor!
EDGAR: Golly! That's odd! [*Pause*] What's the *umbrella stand* doing in here?
POOKIE: I don't know, but I can't possibly play tennis now.
EDGAR: What do you mean, old thingy-poo?
POOKIE: It's the Colonel.
EDGAR: What*ever* is he doing down there?
POOKIE: I rather think he's dead.
EDGAR: Oh yes—does look rather dead doesn't he?

POOKIE: *Ra-ther.*

EDGAR: Eyur! He's covered in blood!

POOKIE: And he's usually so dapper!

EDGAR: Not like him at all is it?

POOKIE: Well, like him a bit, but quieter.

EDGAR: Letting the side down I'd say!

POOKIE: [*Crouches down*] Look! There's a hole in his waistcoat.

EDGAR: [*Down beside her*] So there is—Well *done* me ole thingy-whatsit-poo. That must be how all the blood is getting out. Look, I can get my finger right inside it. Now, what could have caused that, eh?

POOKIE: You pushed it in with your hand.

EDGAR: Yes, no—I mean how did the *hole* come to be there in the first place?

POOKIE: Moths?

EDGAR: Have to be bally vicious, what?

POOKIE: Golly, yes! Great big teeth, great horrid fangs, wicked lips and an evil bitey way of eating.

EDGAR: Look here, I don't know much, but I don't think moths *have* teeth you know.

POOKIE: [*Petulantly*] How do you know? They're so small you couldn't possibly see.

EDGAR: I ... I don't know *how* I know, but I think I *do*. [*Beat*] You're going to have to trust me on that because ... I'm a man, you know.

POOKIE: Ummmm! [*Giggles*]

EDGAR: [*Pause*] Ah!—excuse me, I just have to rearrange my trousers—seem to be all bunched up somehow. [*Stands up*]

POOKIE: Flannel does that sometimes. Shall I help?

EDGAR: [*Hastily*] No, no, very kind and all that, but I've nearly got it—uh, there! That's better.

POOKIE: Oh—you've got blood all over yourself—how beastly horrid.

EDGAR:	Dash it.
POOKIE:	Better take them off and get some cold water on it.
EDGAR:	No, it's gone down now.
POOKIE:	You needn't be shy with me—I've seen ... gentleman's legs before.
EDGAR:	Before what?
POOKIE:	Before ... before other bits of them!
EDGAR:	Crikey!
POOKIE:	Um. Well—off with them!
EDGAR:	Right-ho ... Er, um ... oh, can't seem ...
POOKIE:	[*Wailing*] What is it, why aren't they coming off?
EDGAR:	Er, don't know [*Pause*] never done this before, you know. [*Confidentially*] Jeffers, my man generally takes care of it.
POOKIE:	Can't be *that* difficult, can it? Let *me*. [*Strains*] Uhhh!
EDGAR:	I Don't know, Jeffers is highly trained, what?
POOKIE:	Look, they're quite baggy—perhaps if you breathe in you can just sort of shimmy out of them.
EDGAR:	[*Breathes in—pause*] No-go—there's a lot of shirt inside here—keeps the trousers snickety-poo tight around the ribs you know.
POOKIE:	[*Pause. Snaps her fingers*] I've *got* it—let's see if we can untuck some of that shirt and slacken you off—come on—tug!
EDGAR:	[*Rhythmically with effort*] Uhhh. Uhhh.
POOKIE:	Uhhh. Uhhh.
EDGAR:	Uhh.
POOKIE:	Uhh.
EDGAR:	Wait a minute—I'm pooped. [*Breathing heavily*] Let's sit down.
POOKIE:	[*Pause*] There's a lot of shirt there, isn't there?
EDGAR:	Jermyn Street, you know.
POOKIE:	[*Wails with despair*] Oh, what are we going to do?

EDGAR: There, there, old thing, I expect they'll come off eventually. Tell you what—I'll call Jeffers—he'll know what to do!

POOKIE: Oh well done, I knew you'd come up trumps.

EDGAR: Jeffers! Jeffers! Where is he?

POOKIE: Here, perhaps if you fire this revolver I just found in the coal scuttle, he'll hear it.

EDGAR: Jolly good idea.

SFX Pistol shot, plaster falling from ceiling. Miraculously, Jeffers is there.

JEFFERS: You fired, sir?

EDGAR: Ah, there you are Jeffers—where have you been?

JEFFERS: Ahh ... I was, ahem, cleaning the fluff from the bath plug-holes, sir.

POOKIE: That's not your job, Jeffers, you know; that's for the tweeny to do.

JEFFERS: Ah, hmm, a little hobby of mine, miss; I have an extensive collection of tufts from forty years of service, dating from when I myself was a boot boy in the great house. Er, if I may be so bold—I'd be honoured to show it to you some time, miss.

EDGAR: No you may not, Jeffers, now come and remove my trousers.

JEFFERS: Right away, sir ...

SFX Rustle of heavy material as trousers fall to the floor.

JEFFERS: ... there.

EDGAR: Jeffers—you make it look so easy.

JEFFERS: Thank you, sir ... Er, sir—shall I clear away the, er, body, sir?

POOKIE: Oh, Jeffers, would you? You are a lamb.

EDGAR: [*To Pookie, affectionately*] Baa!

POOKIE: Baa!

JEFFERS:	As you say, miss. I'll get Mrs Figgis to scrub the rug and I'll give your trousers a good soak, sir. Soon have them as good as new.
EDGAR:	Oh don't bother with all that, Jeffers, Throw the bally things away—I've got heaps more.
JEFFERS:	Very well, sir—oh, sir in that case may I suggest to donate them to Mrs Goblin for her cat—it has pneumonia.
EDGAR:	That's absurd, Jeffers, if the cat is *that* ill he'll never survive long enough to grow into them, throw them away!
JEFFERS:	Of course, sir. I'll attend to the body. [*Picks it up, wheezing and groaning*] H-u-u-u-p!

SFX Carrying the body away, stumbling and bashing into furniture, etc.

A moment of silence then Pookie giggles.

EDGAR:	What is it, what are you laughing at?
POOKIE:	Your *legs*—they're so white! [*Giggles*] You ... you don't need to wear your flannels at all!
EDGAR:	Eh? Ha, ha, ha; you're right!
POOKIE:	Do you know what I have a fancy for?
EDGAR:	What?
POOKIE:	To play around with you!
EDGAR:	I say! Anyone for *tennis!* I'll get my racquet. Come on, out into the garden, what fun, I ...

SFX Scuffle and thump as he falls.

EDGAR:	Arghhh!
POOKIE:	Edgar, what happened?
EDGAR:	I tripped on my shirt tails. [*Pathetically*] Ow!—I've scraped my knee, so I can't play now! It's just not fair!

THE END

Noah

(Originally: Waiting for...)

Competition theme: The flood. 2001.
3rd place

I'd read some of the lesser known work of Samuel Beckett before writing this, and assimilated some of his style ... But I was more interested in how Noah was traumatised by events—and the Bible tells how after the Ark washed up, he gets very drunk ... Here, Noah and his Wife happen to have Irish accents.

Characters

NOAH and his WIFE   apparent age late 60s

A drunk, shabby old man with an earthenware jug sits against a rock in the sun.

NOAH: Ooooh!—The stench, never forget the stench—a million different kinds of shit. Times two. "300 cubits by 50 cubits by 30 cubits"—but not a mention about shit management! "A window shalt thou make"—one window to let out all the stink—NOT ENOUGH! Every day you shovel shit and you pray, and you wait and you shovel and still the shit comes. [*He drinks*] Still smell it—don't think I'll ever get that smell out of my head. Oh I tried. Sucked water up my nose, into my head. Nearly drowned! Time in the Flood and I nearly drown washing my nose! [*He drinks*] Nothing to do. No more Voice. No one to tell me.

WIFE: [*Off*] Noah!

NOAH: NO ONE!

WIFE: [*Off*] Noah! Move your lazy arse you useless exhibit!

NOAH: No one, no one, no one can tell me what to do. Didn't I save all the animals—every creeping thing that crawled and galloped and slithered and flapped and shitted, didn't I? Good God.

WIFE: [*Entering*] What are you doing? Nothing. Get up off your flabby arse. There are things.

NOAH: Forget it.

WIFE: Every all day—you tend your vines and drink, drink your wine. You're a holy disgrace!

NOAH: I'm a hero. I'm entitled.

WIFE: You're not a hero now, you're a grubby auld man-wreck.

NOAH: Wreck—maybe. Easy was it? Rounding up all the animals? Getting them into the Ark. Building the Ark. Nearly killed me.

WIFE: Didn't we help you? Me, your sons? To the bone, eh?

	We all did and it was hard, OK? So. But it's done now, the animals are saved; we're saved, thank the Lord. And life goes on. Your sons and daughters-in-law are getting on with their lives.
NOAH:	Having babies.
WIFE:	And? If they don't, there's no one else to do it.
NOAH:	Have a drink.
WIFE:	Certainly not.
NOAH:	Have a drink, you sour faced whinny!
WIFE:	I will not. Where's your self respect?
NOAH:	Up the mountain in that Ark, buried under piles of shit of many kinds!
WIFE:	Will you never shut up about the shit for God's sake? All I hear from you is shit this, shit that, I'm tired of the shit, I'm tired of you.
NOAH:	I'm resting. Leave me alone, woman. Leave me alone.

Defeated, she sits next to him and begins to weep.

NOAH:	Remember? Before, eh? Before the Flood? Our auld house. All gone and gone. Washed away, washed clean, washed up. Don't want to get things dirty again. What makes you think it'll be any better? You come nagging at me to get on and do something but I don't know what to do to make it better. Eh? What do you want?
WIFE:	I'd like a nice house, like our auld little house; that would be nice wouldn't it? I'd like to eat good food. I want a proper home.
NOAH:	What's wrong with God's own sky eh? When it rains we can go under a tree, or in a cave; that's all right.
WIFE:	It's not all right, a house is better than a cave, we're not animals, we're people.
NOAH:	They said I was mad, ha-ha! What are you doing you crazy auld coot, eh? Are you building a boat, eh? Will you carry it to the sea? Ha! Well I've got news for them, I am crazy! I'm crazy and I'm tired.
WIFE:	And I'm tired. I'm worn and weary.

NOAH: Yes. Come on, buck up. Have a drink.

She drinks.

WIFE: Ah, what are we going to do?
NOAH: Come on. [*He puts an arm around her*] Eh? Eh? Ah.
WIFE: All those animals, who'd a thought it?
NOAH: All that shit, who'd a thought that, eh?

She giggles despite herself, subsides.

WIFE: What's to be done?
NOAH: Kind o' house do you want, eh? Hmm? Nice little bedroom? Living room, ballroom? Nice big ballroom? For the dancing, the dancing! Hah! [*He gets up and dances drunkenly about*] Come and dance, come dance with me! Whee! Don't need a ballroom, just dance! Ha-ha!
WIFE: You stupid auld plank!
NOAH: Come and dance!
WIFE: No, you divot.
NOAH: Come on!
WIFE: No. NO!

He stops and stands, sobered.

WIFE: Barnacle brain.
NOAH: Hmm.
WIFE: Stupid auld man.
NOAH: Well, what does it matter, eh? I'm stupid and who's to see and who's to care?
WIFE: If your sons were to see you now, their wives.
NOAH: Don't you worry about them. They're busy repopulating the world, they don't care about me.
WIFE: They do.
NOAH: THEY DON'T!

She sobs.

NOAH: Oh, don't start again, come on. Is that rain? Did I feel

	the rain?
WIFE:	There's not a cloud in the sky!
NOAH:	I felt rain. There, again!
WIFE:	There's no rain, nor will be.
NOAH:	There's rain. There! Feel it?
WIFE:	You're mad!
NOAH:	There's rain, there's rain!
WIFE:	There's no rain!
NOAH:	We'll need a shelter, back to that rotting Ark, here we go again, back to all the shit and the roaring and the lowing and bleating and squawking and squealing and hooting and yelling and rain and rain and rain! RAIN!
WIFE:	Stop it!
NOAH:	You stop it! Stop it—AHHHHHH! [*Crying*] The rain, here's the rain ...

She hugs him.

WIFE:	I see it, I feel it Shhh! Shhh. It's all over now. All over.

At last he subsides. She stoops for the jug.

WIFE:	Here now—have a drink—have some of your own lovely wine.

He drinks. She drinks.

WIFE:	Dance with me.

He's astonished.

WIFE:	You're right. Who's to see? The world is all clean and a bit of dancing won't dirty it up. Come. Come now.

They cling together and sway gently.

THE END

Police Vet

Competition theme: The unexpected. 2001.
1st place and Best Play of the Year

A spoof of the many and various cop shows on TV that I grew up with. If you were going to have a performed reading of this one, the stage directions are very much an important part of the proceedings and should be read out with appropriate gravitas.

Characters

STEPHEN KESTREL	30s, Police Vet
MONA KESTREL	30s, Stephen's wife
MARILYN FINCH	20s, Director of the Zoo
PLANKTON	50s, fish expert
ROY	40s, rival vet
LASSSITER	40s, Head of Reptiles, speaks with an unnatural sibilance

Scene 1. Stephen & Mona's bedroom, night

Darkness. A phone rings.

MONA: [*Sleepy*] Don't answer it.
KESTREL: [*Waking determinedly*] I have to ...

> *He picks up the phone.*

MONA: Stephen do you know what time it is?
KESTREL: It's my job—you should know that by now.
MONA: Your job! What about us?

> *He switches on the light and we see his strikingly handsome face.*

KESTREL: [*Into the phone*] Kestrel. Police vet.

> *Titles and stirring portentous music. POLICE VET. This episode: Tiger Tiger.*

***

Scene 2. The Zoo gates

It's a hell of a night—wind and rain. Stephen Kestrel wearing jeans and anorak pulled hastily over a pyjama top gets out of a car at the zoo gates. He is met by the beautiful Zoo Director, Marilyn Finch. She lets him into the grounds. They talk briskly.

KESTREL: It's late Marilyn—
MARILYN: Stephen, we had another letter ...

> *She shows him a note composed with stuck on letters from a newspaper. It's very messy. Clearly the work of a ... well, a twit. Kestrel snatches it and scans it.*

KESTREL: Why didn't you tell me?
MARILYN: I didn't think you cared.
KESTREL: I care about the animals.

MARILYN: But not about me!
KESTREL: You know I'm married.
MARILYN: Are you just going to pretend nothing happened?

They stop walking.

KESTREL: Look—when we ... [*'had sex' is what he's going to say*]
MARILYN: In with the chimps?
KESTREL: [*Shamefully*] Yes.
MARILYN: They still talk about it.
KESTREL: [*Horrified*] Only between themselves. If my wife finds out, it won't be from them!
MARILYN: [*Defiantly*] I'm having them taught sign language. Once you teach chimpanzees to talk, it's difficult to make them stop!
KESTREL: All right—I admit my marriage is on the rocks—all this running off to see animals at all hours—she doesn't understand!
MARILYN: But I do Stephen. I feel the same way! You and me, what a team we'd make!

A terrible raspberry rings out.

MARILYN: The camel's got dysentery. Fred's in with him.
KESTREL: I can't think about that now. There's a big cat to attend to.

He strides off determinedly. She looks after him with admiration. Another fart followed by a human groan.

***

Scene 3. Zoo buildings interior

Kestrel barges into the tropical fish section which is darkened, but lit by the glow of an enormous illuminated tank full of incredible fish, in which a man in a suit is also casually standing, just because he likes it—hands behind his back, his head and shoulders above the water.

PLANKTON: Ah, Kestrel.
KESTREL: Hello, Plankton. Where's Tandoori now?

PLANKTON: We have her sedated in the operating theatre.

***

Scene 4. Zoo medical bay

A man, Roy, emerges from the operating theatre as Kestrel and Plankton—dripping wet, arrives.

PLANKTON: You know Roy our anaesthetist.

KESTREL: [*Grim*] Hello Roy.

ROY: [*Wary*] Kestrel. She's in here with Lasssiter. We've done what we can for now, but you'd better take a look.

> *They enter a neon-lit space where Lasssiter is attending. He's wearing a snakeskin waistcoat, trousers and boots and has a python wrapped around his shoulders. There's an operating table and upon it is an enormous Bengal tiger, clearly unconscious; it's covered, apart from its head, in a green surgical sheet. They stand back in awe of the creature. Kestrel walks slowly around it.*

KESTREL: What kind of a maniac could harm a creature like this? What kind of a twisted pervert could even contemplate damaging such beauty, such power?

> *Marilyn arrives. Kestrel looks at the stuck together note he still clutches.*

KESTREL: [*Reads*] Tiger tiger burning bright, this will be a kinky night …?

LASSSITER: [*Knowing*] I think you care more about animals than people.

KESTREL: It's my job—it's what I do. [*Beat*] What's wrong? what did the swine do to her?

LASSSITER: [*Testing*] You're the vet—you tell me.

KESTREL: She's properly sedated?

ROY: No she always sleeps like this … [*Irritated*] Of course she's sedated—what do you take me for?

KESTREL: After the incident with the crocodile you can't blame

	me for asking.
ROY:	You always bring that up.
KESTREL:	I could have lost an arm!
LASSSITER:	Gentlemen please!
KESTREL:	[*Pause*] I'm sorry ... right let's take a look ... Now then, how are you old girl? Hmm. small scar on nose: old. Whiskers: a little bent, nothing too serious. Teeth ...

He pulls back the tiger's mouth to see the fangs.

| KESTREL: | Slightly chipped—just what you'd expect of a tiger of this age in captivity; ears, the left a little chewed: old wound. Now then ... |

He pulls the sheet slowly back down the body of the tiger as far as the rear legs. Marilyn controlling her breathing with effort—she strokes her own arm unconsciously—perhaps she remembers when Stephen touched her like that ... He runs his hand expertly along the tiger's front limbs. Everyone is holding their breath.

| KESTREL: | No broken bones. Claws ... perfect. Ow!—and sharp! |

He smiles wryly—it's just a joke, the tension is broken. They all breathe again. He strokes his hand along the mighty beast's body. He listens intently with a stethoscope and grunts with approval.

| KESTREL: | Coat surprisingly bright. |
| MARILYN: | We do know how to look after our animals. |

Reverently, he reveals the rear legs and checks them, and then the pelvis. He tucks his fingers into the groin—purely professionally. He looks away—he doesn't need his eyes—his fingers see well enough.

| KESTREL: | So far so good—are you *sure* this animal has been tampered with? |

Roy lunges at him.

| ROY: | Do you think we got you out on a night like this on a |

	wild goose chase?
KESTREL:	Steady tiger!
PLANKTON:	All right now, let's calm down shall we? We're all professionals.

They all turn to look at Plankton who is standing soaked in a pool of water. There is a little fish flapping on the floor. He picks it up and pops it unself-consciously into his top jacket pocket. They all resume their business. Kestrel pulls the sheet from the tail with a flourish. At the very end of it is a bandage. He looks up sharply:

KESTREL:	What did he do?
MARILYN:	[*Pause*] It's a twist [*Pause*] in the tail!

Close up on the grim face of Kestrel.

***

Scene 5. Zoo buildings interior

Kestrel and Marilyn walking down a corridor. They pass a keeper, a dumpy girl; she is standing bare-footed as she takes lumps of dung from a bucket and drops them into her wellies. They ignore her.

KESTREL:	[*Muttering*] Tiger tiger burning bright, this will be a kinky night—kinky—kink in the tail ... guh!
MARILYN:	It's the fifth letter, but the first time anything has actually happened.
KESTREL:	... Stupid ...
MARILYN:	It's the work of a jealous person.
KESTREL:	What I don't understand is how whoever did this got access, how he—
MARILYN:	Or she.
KESTREL:	Or she, got into the cage and managed to ... [*he does a two handed twisting motion, doing the sound with his mouth*] ... the tail. He—
MARILYN:	Or she.
KESTREL:	Or she, must be someone the tiger knows and trusts ...

	He—
MARILYN:	Or she.
KESTREL:	OR SHE, must work AT THE ZOO. [*Pause*] Who do you know here who is jealous, and a little ... strange?

Kestrel looks thoughtful. Marilyn looks inscrutably at him ...

***

Scene 6. Somewhere in the Primates section

In the dark, a chimp is hunched in a corner. It has a whole load of individual letters cut haphazardly from several newspapers. There is glue, scissors and paper. It is composing a threatening letter and making a real mess of it. The letters are stuck all over its fingers—they won't stick to the page properly. The chimp is getting very worked up. It scrunches up its work, pauses, then turns to a computer and starts to type. As it does so, it stops to furiously wiggle its fingers in sign language. We see subtitles:

"This will show them. They think I'm blind? They think I don't care? Think I don't have feelings?"

It sits back as a page prints out reading: Birds and bees but what about ME?! Chimp does several back flips and screeches.

End music and credits, so fast that mercifully, we can't read them.

THE END

Competition theme: A Touch of Magic. 2002.
2nd place

If you had one wish, what would it be? Set in one cosy scene—a man and a woman together in a cave …

Characters

MILDRED   the woman, any age but a little younger than the man
WIZ   the man

Two people sit on cushions on the floor facing each other, surrounded by drapes and lit by candles. She is immaculate in a tight 1960's dress, patent high-heel shoes with matching handbag and beehive hairdo. He has short hair and wears a sensible Aran cardigan and baggy satin Arabian Nights trousers and curly-toed slippers.

MILDRED: Mildred.

WIZ: Wiz.

They shake hands.

WIZ: Look into my eyes. What do you see?

She leans in.

MILDRED: [*With awe*] I see fire, I see ice ... I see continents colliding, I see dragons, I see galaxies exploding. [*Then ordinary*] The usual.

WIZ: Why are you here? What do you want?

MILDRED: [*Matter of fact*] Love. What does anybody want?

WIZ: Money, power, esteem, fame, excitement. Occasionally, wisdom. Health.

MILDRED: Happiness?

WIZ: No one ever asks for happiness. They assume it comes with the other things.

MILDRED: And does it?

WIZ: Sometimes. but perhaps even magic cannot deliver happiness ...

MILDRED: And love?

WIZ: Love—wish for love and you may get it from someone you despise. Or, give it to someone who will not return it. Magic needs to be handled carefully!

MILDRED: So. [*Beat*] What's the deal?

WIZ: One wish. No corrections, no returns.

MILDRED: And the price?

WIZ: You pay me nothing. Call it altruism if you like, I get pleasure from giving. But—the cost is enormous. The cost to yourself—what you *pay* in terms of your own *emotions*.

MILDRED: I don't understand.

WIZ: Let's say you wish for something, and you end up regretting it. It may even drive you to despair. *That* would be the true cost of what you wished for.

MILDRED: I might also make a good decision, What I wish for might make me feel wonderful, fulfilled, improved.

WIZ: There's always a cost, a hidden charge. Let's say you did choose wisely. What about other people? Perhaps they'd be jealous and hate you for your good fortune. How often have we heard about an unbalanced person destroying someone powerful, successful, happy? There are rock stars, world leaders and ordinary people aplenty who have had their lives senselessly curtailed by others.

MILDRED: Then what about asking for something for someone else. If I were unselfish, the effects may be better?

WIZ: There are no guarantees. Wish anyone something good, and the ripples in the universe may return as a tidal wave. Besides, the magic I offer is only available for the wishee. You have to wish for something for yourself. That's the condition.

MILDRED: Then what's the point?

WIZ: It's a gamble. It's exciting—isn't it? The thought that you can change your life in the click of a finger? Make a dream come true! [*Beat*] Every time you make a decision there are far reaching effects. You can only go forwards, never back. You have to cope with the consequences of your actions. Magic is just a little more instant, a little more dramatic, a little less humdrum. [*Beat*] Do you still want a wish? You could walk away.

MILDRED: Yes ... But then I'd always regret it ...

WIZ: Yes. You spoke of love ...

MILDRED: What about immortality?!

WIZ: What about it?

MILDRED: Would it be a good thing to ask for?

WIZ: No point. We all have it already! Many religions are quite clear on the subject. Life goes on after death. We are reborn. We continue! We have already lived countless lives before—we just don't remember, usually. We'd go mad if we had to manage the memory of all that. The immortality you are thinking of would be a waste—you want to live forever in this life? You would miss out on the lessons and experiences of all that was intended for you. When this life ends, you will once more discover who you've been.

MILDRED: As you speak I know this to be true ... it's weird, I was always so uncertain about things like that ... [*Beat*] You are strange. Are you a man, a human man?

WIZ: Yes.

MILDRED: A real man with feelings, wants, needs?

WIZ: Oh, yes.

MILDRED: Then how can you offer me, or anyone, magic?

WIZ: I've learnt to channel it. It is in the universe, the bones of the universe, the blood of the universe. It flows through all things. It binds, it is all. You cannot separate it and there is nothing without it.

MILDRED: Then I am magic!

WIZ: Now you see it!

MILDRED: Tell me, is there Evil?

WIZ: As a specific force? No.

MILDRED: But bad things happen, people do wicked things. Terrible things ...

WIZ: There is no force of evil.

MILDRED: But there *is*—people suffer. Much is destroyed.

WIZ: Matter is not destroyed, merely redistributed. *Things* get destroyed, and it is sad for us. but others come along to rebuild, create anew. And as we've already discussed, no one ever really dies.

MILDRED: Then you're saying it's all right to kill, to create

	suffering?!
WIZ:	No, I didn't say it's all right, and it pains me deeply. But the universe goes on anyhow.
MILDRED:	Why do people do bad things?
WIZ:	Because they're people. [*Beat*] I don't mean to be glib, but aren't you here for your wish?
MILDRED:	It all seems pointless.
WIZ:	Have a sandwich.
MILDRED:	What?
WIZ:	A sandwich. I have smoked salmon, cream cheese, spicy chicken—they're very good. Low blood-sugar level. Once you've had something to eat you'll feel much better!
MILDRED:	One moment we're talking about important things and now you're talking about sandwiches.
WIZ:	Right now food is the most important thing. Eat.
MILDRED:	I'll have a smoked salmon. [*She takes a bite*] Mm, the bread is lovely and fresh, the salmon's delish! [*Beat*] Maybe I should wish for more of that!

They laugh.

MILDRED:	Hmm, that's better, I feel more cheerful already. This'll go straight to my hips off course! [*Pause*] How long do I have to decide?
WIZ:	The magic is capricious—if you don't decide soon, the opportunity may be lost—which seems a shame after all the time you spent queuing.
MILDRED:	Right from the ground, to the very top of this mountain!
WIZ:	All the way up from the valley?
MILDRED:	Um. Well, OK—here goes ... I wish for ... I wish for ...
WIZ:	Yes?
MILDRED:	I—erm, can I just say something. This isn't the wish.
WIZ:	OK.
MILDRED:	I ...

WIZ: Hm?

MILDRED: Look, would you, erm …

WIZ: Yes?

MILDRED: Would you, erm—I'm so embarrassed—

WIZ: Don't be—it's all right!

MILDRED: Erm, would you, er, would you, like to kiss me?

Pause.

MILDRED: [*Continues now without pausing for his lines*] Oh, God, I—

WIZ: No—

MILDRED: God, I, I, I, forget I said that, OK?

WIZ: Yes, I—

MILDRED: I feel such a fool—

WIZ: No, don't—

MILDRED: I've come all this way to have a wish, a vague idea that I could have something, something out of a fairy tale, a—

WIZ: Yes.

MILDRED: I've come miles. Miles and miles, putting off the decision of what I wanted to wish for, thinking—

WIZ: YES.

MILDRED: —I'd think of something when the time came. [*Beat*] What?

WIZ: Yes. I would like to kiss you. [*Pause*] I would!

MILDRED: You would?

WIZ: Very much.

MILDRED: Oh.

WIZ: Yes.

MILDRED: Oh …

WIZ: Come here …

MILDRED: Oh …

> *They kiss—long lingering, still and silent. Gently, they break off.*

MILDRED: [*Pause*] Magic!

WIZ: Well, that's my wish come true!

And putting forehead to forehead and nose to nose, they smile contentedly.

THE END

To Use the Vernacular

Competition theme: Modern malaprops. 2002.
4th place

Not really about malapropisms—more about nomenclature, though I got away with it in the competition. A bit close to the bone for some in the audience, so beware. An intimate comedy, for sound only (for very good reasons), about sex. These days people talk frankly about sex and intimacy. But not my grand parents' generation …

If this were to be performed live to an audience, they might be invited to close their eyes as though listening to the radio.

Characters

FRED and SYLVIA   both in their 70s, working class, and married to each other for many years

Night time, and Fred and Sylvia are together in bed ...

FRED: [*Weary complaint*] Look it's been a long day, Sylvia.
SYLVIA: Any old excuse!
FRED: Oh, all right. Come on let's get it over and done with.
SYLVIA: Well you might show a bit of enthusiasm—I am your wife!
FRED: Uhmm.
SYLVIA: And what's that supposed to mean?
FRED: Nothing, nothing.
SYLVIA: It means nothing that I'm your wife?!
FRED: You know I don't mean that.
SYLVIA: [*Pause*] You're so ungracious sometimes, just thoughtless, saying nasty things ...
FRED: All right, come on, you know I love you.
SYLVIA: Um. [*Sulking*] Well.
FRED: Come on. [*Beat*] Now, where's this book of yours then—what's it all about?
SYLVIA: [*Sniff*] I got it from the library, it's an Indian book on lovemaking.
FRED: Spice up your love life, eh?! Let's see ... [*Matter of fact*] Oh, yes [*Turns page*] mm-hm [*Turns page*] ah—huh [*Turns page, pause. Flips through whole book*] Right, then. Which one you want to do?
SYLVIA: All of them! Every one! It's about time we got something out of our lives. I want some excitement. Something different. There's people all over India, all over the world doing this, and I want to be one of them—I want us to be two of them.
FRED: Well, let's start with an easy one, shall we?
SYLVIA: All righty. OK. [*Page turning*] What about this one? Here's the picture.

FRED: Hmmm ... Wha's it called?

SYLVIA: [*Reads*] Crouching Tiger, Hidden Gherkin.

FRED: Right. Well are there any instructions how to get into that position?

SYLVIA: No, there don't seem to be ... Oo look, there's his leg, and that's her arm ...

FRED: What's that bit?

SYLVIA: Well, that's her.

FRED: How can that be her?

SYLVIA: Well what else would it be? [*Pause*] Oh, no—you're right, it's him.

FRED: All right [*Bangs his hands together and rubs*], let's be havin' you.

SYLVIA: Aren't you going to take your pyjamas off?

FRED: It's a bit nippy ... Oh, all right. [*Removes them, and not too fast. Then, proudly*] There!

SYLVIA: And your vest.

FRED: Fuss, fuss, fuss. [*Off it comes*] Uhh, ah. [*Sees his socks and goes for them*] Ah!

SYLVIA: No, leave your socks on, I don't want to see your horrible old feet. Now then ... let me get my leg round ... now you, that's it. [*Beat*] No, no, no.

FRED: What? Well, I can't see the picture.

SYLVIA: [*Beat. Passes book*] Here.

FRED: Right. [*Pause*] Well, that's your wrong leg for a start! Here...

SYLVIA: You know I'm not good with diagrams!

FRED: Right—let me take charge. This is man's work!

SYLVIA: You'll be getting your tools out next!

FRED: Shush. Right, now—this leg here, that leg there, this leg over here [*Grunt*] this leg here, this leg—

SYLVIA: We've run out of legs!

FRED: No, you've slipped, come on—put it back.

SYLVIA: Oo, oo, oo!!!

FRED:	Oh, what's the matter now?
SYLVIA:	My arthritis, don't be so rough! Great big hands. I bruise easy, y' know.
FRED:	Sorry. Right here we go, grab hold of me here, I put my arm here and ... Voila!
SYLVIA:	[*Pause*] Is that right?
FRED:	Yep, just like the picture! Smile!
SYLVIA:	[*Pause*] Well what happens now?
FRED:	Aren't you enjoying it? Wiggle about a bit.
SYLVIA:	[*She tries*] Uh, uh. [*Breathless*] I can't move.
FRED:	Gis a kiss!

3 rather noisy kisses.

SYLVIA:	Well we could have a kiss the usual way.
FRED:	Well it was your idea. Want to try another one?
SYLVIA:	This can't be all there is to it.
FRED:	[*Pause*] Should we have sex?
SYLVIA:	Oh, all right.
FRED:	Come on then. [*Beat*] Let's get untangled.

Exertion.

SYLVIA:	Ooo, ooo, my leg's gone to sleep! No! Careful! Ow! You kicked me! Get your knee out of my ribs. Ouch! And I don't want that in my face, thank you!
FRED:	These old bed springs were never made for this!
SYLVIA:	Clumsy brute!
FRED:	Well, I'm trying to move my arm, you're on my arm— get off you lump!
SYLVIA:	Don't you call me a lump, you're as much a lump as I am.
FRED:	Ouch ... Oooh ... uh! That's got it—roll over. Aagh!

He crashes to the floor. Pause.

SYLVIA:	Oo, Fred are you all right?

He clambers back in bed.

FRED: Oo, your lovely dimpled bum!

He gives it pit-a-pat slaps.

SYLVIA: [*Giggles*] Stop that!

FRED: Oo, you're lovely, I love all of ya! Where's me old man? There he goes, come on. You like him don'tcha? Don'tcha, eh?

SYLVIA: Fred, Fred, stop.

FRED: Ooooh!

SYLVIA: FRED!

FRED: [*Stopping*] What?

SYLVIA: I want to say. I don't like it when you call it that.

FRED: What?

SYLVIA: An "old man". I don't like to think of an old man in bed with us.

FRED: What? [*Pause*] Well, you've never complained before.

SYLVIA: Well, I've never liked it.

FRED: You've never liked it?! You never liked my old—

SYLVIA: The name I mean.

FRED: [*Pause*] Well, what should I call it? Me todger, me willie, me snake?

SYLVIA: It's not much of a snake.

Silence.

SYLVIA: It's nice, but it's not much of a snake. Euch! I wouldn't like a snake. [*Beat*] Don't sulk.

FRED: Well, what should I call it? You tell me!

SYLVIA: Call it by its proper name.

FRED: Proper name? Dick?

SYLVIA: No!

FRED: Cock?

SYLVIA: NO!

FRED:	Prick?
SYLVIA:	No, no. [*Pause*] You know what it's called.
FRED:	Say it then.
SYLVIA:	[*Clinical*] Penis.
FRED:	[*Distastefully*] Penis. That's why there's all the other names.
SYLVIA:	There's all those names cos when we was young it was dirty. You were ashamed to use proper names. Well. I'm not ashamed no more. I like it. I want to be honest.
FRED:	You sure?
SYLVIA:	Yes.
FRED:	All right! [*Pause, then In quick succession*] Penis, penis, penis, penis. [*Beat*] That's not so bad. Come on, gis a cuddle. [*Posh, and getting intimate*] Madam, let me put my penis in your … (!)
SYLVIA:	Yes?
FRED:	Your …
SYLVIA:	Yes, yes?
FRED:	Your—
SYLVIA:	They say it now.
FRED:	Come on …
SYLVIA:	No. Say it!
FRED:	Come on!
SYLVIA:	No, no—not until you say it.
FRED:	I can't.
SYLVIA:	SAY it.
FRED:	No!
SYLVIA:	Say it!
FRED:	COME ON!
SYLVIA:	Not until you say it!
FRED:	I CAN'T.
SYLVIA:	You can!
FRED:	I CAN'T, YOU STUPID CUNT!

        Silence.

SYLVIA: [*Horrified whisper*] What did you call me?

FRED: Oh, God I'm sorry. I'm sorry, I'm sorry—I didn't mean it. You know I didn't. I ... I love you, you know that. Sylvie, doll ... [*Big pause, then quietly*] Vagina. [*Pause*] Sylvie?—vagina. There—I said it. I'd do anything for you girl, you know I would. Sylvie, for God's sake. Vagina vagina vagina vagina vagina vagina vagina.

SYLVIA: [*Beat, then with sorrow and forgiveness*] Oh, Fred.

FRED: Sylv?

        They hug. A quiet kiss.

FRED: I'm sorry, doll.

SYLVIA: I know. [*Beat*] Hug me Fred.

        Breathing.

FRED: I do love you, girl.

SYLVIA: [*Reproachfully, but with love*] Penis.

FRED: Yeh. [*Beat*] 'Ere ... when d'you want to do them other positions, eh?

SYLVIA: Shhhhh!

        Rustle of bedclothes—quiet and intimate.

SYLVIA: Ooo, Fred. Ooo, Freddie. [*Pause. Whispers*] Penis!

FRED: [*Whispers*] Vagina!

THE END

Death of a Writer

Competition theme: It was the writing course that changed my life, wasn't it? 2002.
2nd place

So, you want to be a writer? Famous maxim: write about what you know. Oh, you want to write about spies, space and cowboys ... Well, you might try going on a writing course ...

Characters

MAN	40, a blank canvas
AMANDA	30, nearly beautiful
VICAR	60s, genuine
GINCHLEY	70s, male, academic idiot
LEMONIE	(pronounced Le-mO-ni) 60s, female, posh, excited by the banal
ANDY	20s, a lad

England, the present. A bleak moor. A man in a long black coat is tending a bonfire. In the distance, a small stone church from which a vicar approaches.

VICAR:	You seem troubled—do you want to talk?
MAN:	[*Flat*] Where to start?
VICAR:	[*Compassionate*] Wherever you want. [*Gently*] Who are you?
MAN:	I was a shoe shop manager. I knew all about shoes and feet—but what I really wanted, was to write movies! I wanted to spin exciting nail-biting suspense-laden cliff-hanging tales. Stories of spies, bank robbers and adventurers. But, I couldn't do it ... Oh I could think up the plots, the story lines ... But my characters didn't have that *je ne sais quoi*, that edge of derring-do. You see, *I* was not one to take risks. Not the type to attract the ladies. *I* was not *dangerous*.
VICAR:	[*Warily*] So ... what then?
MAN:	It was the writing course that changed my life. Just one week—residential in a big old house in the country, far away from my ... world of shoes. To be surrounded by a committed and eager band of fellow writers was a heady prospect.
VICAR:	How did it go?
MAN:	Well in many ways it was a bit of a disaster. The key speaker who'd written an Oscar winning screenplay turned out to be alcoholic. All he could do was sob and mutter that Hollywood had destroyed him. And several other billed speakers fell ill apparently, and never turned up.
VICAR:	And what about your fellow writers?
MAN:	A strange bunch. It was clear to me that none of them would ever be real writers. They just didn't have it. And they were never going to get it no matter how many courses they went on. I would have packed up and

gone home, but for one speaker—a young woman. Her name: Amanda Smith. She wasn't well known. Hadn't won any awards for her writing; but it seemed to me she knew her bunions. I mean, onions.

Flashback to the writing course: Inside a study room in a big house with a view of the estate—the late afternoon sun slanting in through tall windows. Amanda is talking to about 9 assorted oddballs. And our man, in horrible brown shoes.

AMANDA: Any questions so far?

A very old man puts up his hand.

AMANDA: Yes?

GINCHLEY: I am writing a screenplay based on a series of books. A series that most of us are familiar with—at least, in part—but, that no one, that I am aware, has read all the way through—that is, in their totality. For me, these books—so far untapped, have concealed within their soft covers, the inspiration for millions, nay billions of stories of every possible type and genre; and the film I intend to write from them, will have the largest cast of any ever made.

AMANDA: How fascinating. What are these books if I may ask?

GINCHLEY: The London Telephone Directory.

AMANDA: [*Bemused*] Your question?

GINCHLEY: How do I stop people stealing my idea?

AMANDA: [*Beat*] I believe there will be a talk on copyright later in the week. Let's move on shall we—to an area that Mr—?

GINCHLEY: Ginchley.

AMANDA: Mr Ginchley in particular, will probably find very beneficial. That of *character development*.

MAN: [*To the vicar*] She went on to describe a simple technique that if carried through with imagination and attention to detail, would give imagined characters a dense internal reality which would make our stories rich and compelling.

AMANDA: Your homework is to create a biography for your leading character. You must know everything about them. [*Dreamily*] Ask yourself if 'he' is suave, dashing, brave, dangerous, spontaneous ...

MAN: [*To the Vicar*] I set to that evening to create my ideal fictional hero. I considered every detail of his life—from his birth and education, his loves, triumphs, failures—an *authentic* hero has to have failures—what he liked to eat, sexual predilections—

VICAR: My word!

MAN: —in fact every single aspect of his life up until now—where my screenplay would start. By the time I had finished, I had filled 40 odd pages, and felt I knew him better than I knew myself. I had before me the blueprint for a thrilling adventurer—a man who could take us on a journey out of our humdrum lives to the very depths of the soul.

Study room, the next day.

AMANDA: [*With relish*] Right, let's have a taste of some of these characters. Where's Mr Ginchley, does anybody know?

LEMONIE: He told me he wasn't feeling very well—something about a creative block.

AMANDA: Oh dear, well let's carry on without him. Do *you* have a character you can tell us about?

LEMONIE: Yes, I do. Your talk has been a great inspiration. I have been able to add a great deal of pith to my writing. My character's name is Lemonie Fustian. She is 67, she likes knitting, and her speciality [*With relish*] is real egg custard.

AMANDA: [*Kind*] It's a start ... consider her childhood, some of her formative experiences.

LEMONIE: Ah. [*She scribbles in a notebook while muttering grumpily*] Quite unnecessary, I know my character as I know myself.

AMANDA: Anyone else? Andy.

ANDY: My character is Stella. She can take on any shape, but mostly, she looks like Jennifer Lopez. Clothes are an

	alien concept to her because, well, she's an alien ...
MAN:	[*To the Vicar*] And so it went on. These people had learnt nothing. I held back to the end. I could see Amanda was wilting. I spoke.
MAN:	[*To Amanda, cool and confidant*] The name's Charles, Charles Sterling ... but enough of me. You look like you could do with a break. What do you say we get out of here? Let me show you some of the sights. The view from the lake is stunning; and then—a champagne picnic in the shade of the rose garden.
AMANDA:	[*As in a dream*] How lovely, yes ...
MAN:	[*To the Vicar*] And together, arm in arm, we strolled out of the class leaving those fools blinking in the dusty air. What had come over me? This wasn't me—my name's Edwin. I had been speaking as my character; I had become *him!*

Later, in bed.

AMANDA:	This is crazy, Charles—I don't know anything about you, except you are the most exciting man I ever met at a writing course; that I ever met anywhere! In horrible shoes!
MAN:	Shut up and kiss me.

They kiss.

MAN:	Together we can do anything. Have you ever been to the Far East? Let me take you. It's damned exciting!
AMANDA:	When?
MAN:	Right now!
AMANDA:	But, the class ...
MAN:	You really want to stay at this fusty old place, when you could be swimming in perfumed tropical seas and sampling exquisite cuisine from around the world?
AMANDA:	But why me?
MAN:	Because—you are a fascinating, vibrant, beautiful woman; and I love you with all my heart, passion and breath.

AMANDA: [*Flip*] Well when you put it like that. [*Beat, serious*] I would die for you.

Daytime. Dressed in black chic, they burst into a bank. He holds his black gloved hands as though they are a gun.

MAN: Everyone down! Like starfish!

AMANDA: Now!

All the customers drop instantly. Amanda whacks the security cameras with a severed parking meter. She holds out two bags to the terrified cashiers.

MAN: Fill them—come on!

AMANDA: Kiss me!

They kiss.

In a car travelling fast, pursued by flashing lights and sirens—he drives, she laughs wildly. Bank notes flutter all around.

AMANDA: Kiss me!

They kiss.

Underwater: He and she in rubber suits and aqualungs swim side by side through blue tropical ocean amidst coral and stripy fish.

AMANDA: [*Sounds like blowing through a straw into a glass of water*] Bubble bubble!

They kiss.

The present.

VICAR: What an extraordinary story. I suppose you are sad now because you realise your folly ... your sins.

MAN: Not at all. I'm sad because of the funeral. The funeral of someone I used to love very much. Someone who died so that I could live.

VICAR: Oh no ... surely not—? [*Beat*] Would you like me to say a few words?

MAN:	That would be nice.
VICAR:	Dear Lord, we beseech you, take the soul of Amanda to your everlasting—
MAN:	*No!* No: Edwin. The funeral was for *my past.*
	On to the smouldering heap, he tosses a pair of horrible brown shoes. A Lamborghini pulls up, the doors open like angel's wings revealing Amanda. He gets in, they kiss, the doors close and the car slides away. The Vicar watches it recede.
VICAR:	[*Stunned, and a little envious*] Amen.

THE END

Gumpy Forever

Competition theme: Every picture tells a story. 2004.
3rd place

Black comedy about life, death, bullying and art. George, Edith and Bunty seem to have stepped out of a strange Enid Blyton novel. And Gumpy, out of a nightmare.

Characters

GEORGE	a young man
EDITH	a young woman with blonde hair
BUNTY	a young woman, not blonde
GUMPY	a big fat greasy nasty man, the landlord

To be played earnestly, naively, but sincerely.

Scene 1

Lights up: A plain, drab living room in a flat. Two armchairs, two dining chairs and a coffee table. Upstage right, door to hall. Upstage left, door to kitchen. George & Edith are sitting in sad silence. Edith looks around the room.

EDITH: [*Sigh*] If we had some lovely art, we'd be happier.

GEORGE: It takes more than art to make you happy.

Bunty enters from the hallway, holding a letter.

BUNTY: Look.

EDITH: Oh, no.

GEORGE: Oh, that horrid man, why won't he leave us alone?

EDITH: He knows we're frightened of him.

GEORGE: Huh, lumpy Gumpy.

BUNTY: George!

GEORGE: I'm not frightened of *him*.

EDITH: [*Quietly*] Yes you are.

GEORGE: What's he say now?

BUNTY: Here, you read it. I'm all dizzy.

GEORGE: Right, let's see. [*Reading to himself*] Hmm, hmmm, ahh, oh … d, d, d, signed, "Arthur G. P. W. Gumpy. PS: HAR, HAR!" … The swine!

EDITH: Read it.

GEORGE: I did.

EDITH: Read it.

GEORGE: I did.

EDITH: READ IT READ IT READ IT READ IT READ IT. ALOUD. ALL OF IT!

GEORGE: All right, calm down. Right.

BUNTY: Read it, George!

GEORGE: I'm reading it ... Ahem, "Dear my tenants, how are you? I'm fine. I have made a decree: William must go, filthy beggar. I will come today any time and if he is not gone by eating, I will cut off the ears of the blondie one."

EDITH: [*Covering her ears protectively*] OH!

GEORGE: New sentence: "Eat him up!" Despicable. Well, who's to eat William?

EDITH: I will have to, it's my ears he'll chop off.

GEORGE: Yes.

BUNTY: No! How can you be so mean, George? *You* must eat William.

GEORGE: Eugh!

EDITH: Oh, would you George? For me?

GEORGE: No, why should I?

BUNTY: You're so mean, George. Don't you like Edith's ears?

GEORGE: They're all right, but ...

EDITH: But what?

GEORGE: [*To Edith*] You don't need them. [*To Bunty*] She doesn't need them.

BUNTY: Of course she needs them.

GEORGE: She doesn't. Look, you could put your hair down—and no one would ever know they'd gone. Like my toes.

BUNTY: Rubbish, it's not like toes at all! Anyway, he did you a favour by cutting them off: now you take children's size shoes and they're much cheaper, you should be grateful.

GEORGE: I'm not eating William. That's it.

BUNTY: Get William.

GEORGE: No!

Edith goes, and returns with a small square cage and puts it on a table.

EDITH: Here he is, Bunty.

The two women peer into the cage.

BUNTY: [*Sweetly*] Ahhh! Bye bye William. [*Businesslike*] Eat him George.

GEORGE: No!

She grabs George's right arm with both her hands.

BUNTY: I've got him, Edith.
GEORGE: Let go!
EDITH: Open wide!
GEORGE: I will not!

Edith picks up the cage and presses it against George's face.

EDITH: Gahhh!
BUNTY: Take him out of the cage first!
GEORGE: Look, stop, stop.

They desist.

GEORGE: I *will* eat William, all right? But there's no hurry. We'll wait for old Gumpy and I'll just slip him down my throat then.

GUMPY: [*Off*] I'm co-o-o-ming!

BUNTY: Ooh, he's here. Get William out, Edith. Come on George!

Edith gets the mouse from the cage.

GEORGE: No, I've changed my mind, I'm not going to do it.
EDITH: I've got William.
BUNTY: Don't struggle George, succumb.

Edith holds William under George's nose.

EDITH: Suck him down!
GEORGE: Eugh!
EDITH: Suckety-suck!
GUMPY: [*Off*] I'm co-o-o-ming.

BUNTY:	He's in the hall!
EDITH:	Open up, George.
GEORGE:	I shan't, I'm not going to open my—

Edith thrusts the mouse in, and puts her hand over his mouth and keeps it there.

GUMPY:	[*Off*] I'm coming!
EDITH:	Swallow, swallow, swallow!
BUNTY:	Swallow, George, swallow!
GEORGE:	Mmmph!
GUMPY:	[*Off*] I'm coming and I've got my knife!
EMILY:	He's got his knife! Come on George, do it for me.
GEORGE:	Mmmph!
BUNTY:	Yes, do it for Edith, her ears are lovely!
EDITH:	Yes. George, don't be so selfish, just swallow, swallow, swallow!
GEORGE:	Mmmph!

Gumpy's shadow on the wall, knife in hand. They are all terrified.

BUNTY:	Ooh, quick, George, look, here he comes!

Enter Gumpy with large knife.

GUMPY:	I'm here!
GEORGE:	Mmmmmmmm! [*Big swallow*]
GUMPY:	[*Pause*] Who'd have thought it?

Lights down.

***

Scene 2

Lights up: George is sitting on a plain chair, subdued and queasy. Gumpy is sitting in an armchair. The women sit meekly each side of him giving him a manicure.

GUMPY:	What did he taste like? Eh?

GEORGE:	Sort of earthy. He wiggled all the way down. I think he's still wiggling. I think he's swimming around.
EDITH:	Perhaps he's holding his breath.
BUNTY:	How long *can* a mouse hold its breath?

Gumpy gets a large kitchen clock out of his jacket.

GUMPY:	Let's find out, shall we? Tell me when he stops wiggling.

Pause.

GUMPY:	Well?
GEORGE:	It's hard to tell ... *That* was a wiggle! So was that. Though it might just be my innards twitching. Ooooooh ...
GUMPY:	Well?
GEORGE:	Stopped.

They all fall to silence and stillness. Gumpy looks dubiously at the clock. He gives it a shake and regretfully puts it back in his jacket.

EDITH:	Maybe he's playing dead, just pretending.
GEORGE:	Oh!
BUNTY:	What is it?
GEORGE:	OH!
EDITH:	What is it?
GEORGE:	Ooooooooooooooooooooooooooh!

He runs into the kitchen.

GEORGE:	[*Off.* Retching

Pause. George re-enters.]

GEORGE:	He *was* dead.
GUMPY:	I must go.
BUNTY:	[*Formally*] Good-bye.
EDITH:	[*Formally*] Good-bye.
GUMPY:	Hmph.

He shuffles off. They sit in silence.

GEORGE: Stupid old Gumpy.
EDITH: Shhh.
GEORGE: He's gone now. Huh! He's stupid.
BUNTY: He's mean.
GEORGE: William's not dead. He *was* holding his breath! He popped right out and lay in the sink, then he got up and ran about.
EDITH: Oh, William!
GEORGE: I'll go and rinse him off and get him.
BUNTY: Hurry!

George goes off. Sound of running water.

BUNTY: Oh, I'm so relieved.
EDITH: Oh, lovely little William.
BUNTY: Clever little thing.
EDITH: Oh!
BUNTY: Oh!
EDITH & BUNTY: Ahhhhh!

Sound of WASTE DISPOSAL UNIT. Pause. George comes in shamefaced. They look at him. He shakes his head.

BUNTY: You ... murderer.
GEORGE: It was an accident.
EDITH: You brute!
GEORGE: That gives me an idea.
BUNTY: Ssssssss!
GEORGE: Listen to me! I'm going to kill Gumpy.
BUNTY: He's done nothing to me.
EDITH: It's only a matter of time.

Lights down.

***

Scene 3

Lights up: On a side table, a chopping board with various vegetables. Gumpy is sitting in the armchair. The women are at each side as before.

George stands facing Gumpy.

GEORGE: [*Boldly*] It's a dreadful shame, Mr Gumpy.

GUMPY: About what?

GEORGE: Your poor old blunt knife.

GUMPY: My knife's not blunt as well you know. Chop, chop, chop, no toeses!

GEORGE: That's just it. I'll bet my toes blunted your knife.

Gumpy, from an inside jacket pocket, takes out his knife and looks at it.

GEORGE: Let me sharpen it for you, Mr Gumpy.

GUMPY: OH HO! You think I'd give you my knife? I'm not stupid.

GEORGE: I bet you couldn't cut these vegetables really thin, really finely, with that blunt old knife.

GUMPY: Give me those vegetables, I'll show you how finely I can cut them up!

George places the board across the arms of Gumpy's chair.

GEORGE: Carrots.

Gumpy's knife flashes through them.

GUMPY: Chop chop choppety chop!

GEORGE: Not bad. Parsnips.

GUMPY: Chop chop chop chop chop.

GEORGE: Pretty good. Onions.

GUMPY: Chop chop chop.

GEORGE: Could be finer.

GUMPY: CHOP CHOP CHOP.

GEORGE: Finer still.

GUMPY:	CHOP CHOP CHOP CHOP. [*Sniff*]
GEORGE:	Even finer.

More slowly now.

GUMPY:	Chop [*Sob*] chop [*Sob*] chop [*Sob*].
GEORGE:	Why, Mr Gumpy, how can you see to finish, through all those tears? Let me finish the job.
GUMPY:	Here.
GEORGE:	Thank you Mr Gumpy.

George takes the knife and pushes it right into Gumpy's chest. A shocking moment of stillness.

GUMPY:	[*Sobs, looks down*] I know when I'm not wanted.

Gumpy expires.

EDITH:	[*Shocked*] GEORGE. [*With admiration*] You are clever!
BUNTY:	What shall we do we do with him?

Lights down.

***

Scene 4

Lights up: George, Bunty and Edith are sitting quietly but happily in their living room—there is now a Damien Hirst style tank containing Gumpy—pickled. They beam at each other.

EDITH:	You see? All you need's a nice bit of art to make you feel happier.

They gaze at the "art" and nod.

Blackout.

THE END

Stockings, Glimpsed

Competition theme: A glimpse of stocking. 2005.
1st place

The competition title suggests the "olden days" when a lady's ankle might drive a chap wild with desire; but there are different ways to wear stockings ... This has a modern-day setting. I pictured this as film, though when first performed, it worked a treat with the scene descriptions simply spoken aloud.

Characters

TIM	30s, naïve, good hearted	
WANDA	stern but sweet	} these three women,
BARB	hard as nails	} triplets,
SARAH	sad demeanour	} early 30s, dark hair
MAN	disgruntled customer	
POLICEMAN	40s, authoritative	

For a simple read, actors stand (even when the script suggests sitting, etc).

I suggest one actor to play the triplets, and I suggest modifying the voice according to character traits (see above), and when in the car, face front and adjust your position accordingly: Barbara, is the driver. For Sarah, shift sideways left to front passenger position. Wanda is in the rear behind Barbara, next to Tim also in the rear (who's behind Sarah, and he should stay in that position).

The Policeman uses a bullhorn—I suggest just cupping hands to mouth.

Interior, bank.

TIM: [*To audience*] My first view of her was from the floor, so chiefly it was her boots that I found myself looking at. Black and elegant. She kicked me viciously in the ribs with one of them as I lay there ... Though I usually like to see who's kicking me, I did not feel inclined to look up at that moment. Under the circumstances.

WANDA: [*Loud and dangerous*] No one move!

TIM: And no one did. Natural authority. Marvellous. On the deck with me: six or seven customers I'd say. Men, women of various ages. Carpet a bit grubby—

WANDA: Stay down!

TIM: —but there you are: nothing that wouldn't brush off.

I couldn't really see what was going on, but there were three of them—all in black. Stockings ... pulled over their heads. Guns of course. Shotguns, I presume, but I'm not an expert.

They—the gang—seemed pretty efficient.

I heard the security door open, the rustle of sacks ...

Everything seemed to be going fine—from their point of view.

I rolled over to get a better view. That was when she

WANDA:	kicked me.
WANDA:	Down, boy!
TIM:	Such authority. [*To Wanda*] Do you need a hostage?
WANDA:	Shut up, stay quiet!
TIM:	Because if you do, I'd like to volunteer.
WANDA:	What?
TIM:	I think you're doing a very fine job. Cool, organised. I like that. I'd like to help. [*To audience*] Someone near me on the floor, an elderly lady I think, made that clicking, disapproval noise with her tongue on the back of her teeth. Tch tch tch.
WANDA:	Shut it old woman!
TIM:	And she kicked her, but not too hard I think.
WANDA:	So you want to be my hostage do you?
TIM:	[*To Wanda*] Yes please. [*To audience*] Frankly I was surprised at myself. It's not the sort of thing I normally do ... She pointed her gun at my head, pushed it against my temple.
WANDA:	We don't. Take. Hostages.
TIM:	[*To Wanda*] Can't you make an exception? I'd make a good hostage, really I would. I'd be no trouble.
WANDA:	[*Sarcastic*] I'll bear it in mind.
TIM:	Thanks. [*To audience*] Then they were leaving.
WANDA:	Stay down or we'll blow your brains out!
TIM:	And they were gone. I was disappointed. I got up immediately and went over to the glass door. She was outside on the pavement. The other two were already in their car. She saw me. [*Hopefully, to Wanda*] Hostage. [*To audience*] She shook her head, jumped in the car and whoosh, they were gone. I looked around. The people on the floor were looking up at me with what can only be described as disapproval. I decided to leave.
MAN:	Don't you dare leave—the police are going to want to talk to you.

TIM: —Said one man.

Distant police sirens. Nearby screech of tyres.

TIM: I looked outside. The robbers' car was back again! The rear door of the car opened and a black-clad arm beckoned frantically in my direction. [*To Man*] Sorry. [*To audience*] I said, and ran for the car.

WANDA: Come on, get in, hostage!

TIM: I did. She called from the open window:

WANDA: [*Shouting*] Don't come after us or we'll kill the hostage!

Car door slams. Screech of tyres. Roar of acceleration.

TIM: I was suffused by a warm glow. It felt good to be wanted. Though I suppose, in the technical sense, they were "wanted" more than I. The car tore through the town centre still pursued by the police.

Sirens.

BARB: It's not working—show them we mean business!

TIM: The driver—also a woman!

Car door opens.

WANDA: Back off or I'll throw him out!

TIM: She hung me out of the door as we sped along. What a thrill. I felt her strong hands gripping me and I felt … safe.

Sirens cut as pursuit ends.

WANDA: [*Grunting with effort as she pulls him back inside*] Uuuh!

Door shuts.

TIM: Whew! That was invigorating! I'm Tim.

WANDA: [*Sullen*] Hello Tim.

BARB: [*Sarcastic*] Hi.

Pause.

SARAH: [*Sad*] All right?

TIM: [*To audience*] All three: women! I noticed for the first time that they'd removed their stocking masks. The one beside me who'd held me out of the car was stunning, lovely eyes, dark hair. The other two had dark hair also, but I could only see the backs of their heads.

TIM: [*To them*] Well done. You were splendid. Bravo! Glad I could help. In these days of apathy and gross inefficiency, it's refreshing to see such enthusiasm and frankly, sheer professionalism. [*To audience*] Very soon we were out in the country. [*To them*] Just drop me off anywhere.

WANDA: We can't do that. You've seen us now.

TIM: No, not true, I've actually only seen one of you, and though you're unusually beautiful, I promise I will not reveal a thing to the authorities. [*To audience*] The one in the front passenger seat turned to face me. [*To them*] Well, I never ... [*To audience*] Then I caught a glimpse of the third one, the driver, in her mirror. [*To them*] I'll be ...! Identical triplets!

Sound of a low flying helicopter.

BARB: Dammit!

WANDA: Keep going!

TIM: How much do you think you got away with?

BARB: [*Driving wildly*] Shut up and mind your own business.

WANDA: We're hoping for about 100,000.

TIM: £100,000! Phew. What do you want it for?

SARAH: Cosmetic surgery.

TIM: But you don't need surgery, you're beautiful, you're all beautiful, all of you are.

SARAH: It's hell! Either men are intimidated by us, or they're obsessed by us, or—

WANDA: We just want to be different, that's all.

POLICEMAN: [*Bullhorn from helicopter*] This is the police! Stop the car!

TIM:	But why do you need to steal? You could get lots of money from modelling, I'm sure.	
WANDA:	We don't want to be models, we're intellectuals.	
POLICE:	[*Bullhorn*] Stop the car, you can't escape!	
TIM:	I see your point. What a curse. To be so beautiful, and identical. And yet, unique.	
WANDA:	People are freaked out—all they can do is gawk and blurt and point. We're hardly treated as human.	
BARB:	So we're all going to have surgery.	
TIM:	Surely ... only two of you need to change your appearance.	
SARAH:	That wouldn't be fair.	
TIM:	It doesn't seem right. Usually people have surgery to try to make themselves better looking, but you—	
SARAH:	They're landing!	
TIM:	It just seems wrong somehow.	
BARB:	They're blocking the road!	

Squeal of brakes.

POLICEMAN:	[*Bullhorn*] Come on out with your hands up or we'll open fire!
WANDA:	[*Shouting from car window*] You can't shoot us we've got a hostage!
POLICEMAN:	[*Bullhorn*] We're Special Branch so we don't care!
SARAH:	[*Shouting*] But an innocent person might get hurt!
TIM:	[*To them*] I'm not that innocent.
POLICEMAN:	[*Bullhorn. Derisively*] Yeah, yeah!
BARB:	[*Shouting*] You're bluffing! We will shoot him!
POLICEMAN:	[*Bullhorn*] Then we'll definitely shoot you.
TIM:	What are you going to do?
BARB:	We'll go out in a hail of bullets, there's nothing left!—Yeah?
WANDA:	Yeah!
SARAH:	[*Beat. Sadly*] All right then.

TIM:	Wait! [*Beat*] Send me out, you've got nothing to lose. Maybe I can negotiate.
BARB:	Oh ... all right then, if you must.
WANDA:	Good luck.
TIM:	[*Shouts*] Don't shoot!—I'm coming out! I'm the hostage, I'm unarmed! [*To audience*] To cut a long story short, they were policemen in need of love and understanding. And the triplets were desperate for genuine affection. They couldn't help falling for each other.
	In court, the Judge and jury were so amazed by the triplets, they got off.
	And me?
	Well, I scooped a sizeable reward.
	Which I shared—with the triplets—and the two policemen—just two policemen in the helicopter. Barb and Sarah liked them. I liked Wanda.

Wanda joins Tim, affectionately taking his arm.

TIM:	This is Wanda. [*Modestly*] She was impressed by my bravery.
	And I'm just waiting now for the money to come through—from the film rights. To pay for some cosmetic surgery—just for myself.

Wanda nods. They look lovingly at each other.

THE END

No Business Like It

Competition theme: The mouse, the bitch and the bathrobe. 2009.
1st place

Of all the competition themes ever set at Player Playwrights, this must be the most bizarre ... So, imagine if a certain very famous cartoon mouse was real—and very badly behaved; although, he's not the only one. The other character is a cow, and there's mention of a duck. But what about the elephant in the room? This was written before the Me Too movement became widely known, but I think it's clear that Clara can look after herself ...

Characters

MICKEY   old but feisty, a classic American vaudevillian. Speaks with a gritty voice destroyed/enhanced by a lifetime of cigars and booze. Happens to be a (human-sized) mouse

CLARA   20s, American, beautiful and sexy and she knows it. Happens to be a(n anthropomorphised) cow

Mickey is sitting in his theatre dressing room, a bathrobe carelessly draped around his naked body. He's wiping pan stick make-up from his face, revealing his natural complexion with wrinkled, saggy skin and a nose that's huge and swollen. Lastly he cleans his enormous round circular ears that grow from the top of his head. There's a tentative knock at the door.

MICKEY: Come in if you're beautiful. Stay out if you've got a big yellow beak, a stoopid damn sailor costume, and stinkin' feathers, you scene stealin' short tempered FUCK.

A short pause and the door opens. A very pretty young cow with cute little horns, a low-cut shortie frock and an enormous bust sticks her head around the door.

CLARA: Are you busy, Mr Mouse?

MICKEY: Woah! Never too busy for a lil' cutie like you. Come in, come in. Say—you're *built*.

CLARA: Thank you. I just saw the show—you were great! I'm Clara, I'm an actress …

She slides into the small room.

MICKEY: Man, lookit those mammaries. Are they real?

CLARA: Oh they're real, Mr Mouse, only—

MICKEY: Mickey, call me Mickey, only what?

CLARA: Only, well …

MICKEY: Only only. Come an' sit on my lap you little cutie.

CLARA: Well if you're sure—

MICKEY: Sure? Course I'm sure! Snuggle up!

She gets ready to sit.

CLARA: All right. [*Seductively*] Moo! You ready?

MICKEY: I'm *ready*.

She sits.

MICKEY:	Ai, yai, yai!
CLARA:	Am I hurting you?

She is!

MICKEY:	No, no. Ooh! Ooh! Just ... [*Hoarse*] You're a handful ...
CLARA:	Flatterer!
MICKEY:	Yeah. Yeah ... [*In pain*] Maybe you—
CLARA:	Shall I sit on the stool next to you?
MICKEY:	Yeah! Yeah—good idea. [*Sigh of relief*] That's better. Nice 'n cosy. Quite a relief.
CLARA:	Yeah.
MICKEY:	You were sayin'?
CLARA:	Hmm?
MICKEY:	About your, your décolletage?
CLARA:	Hmm?
MICKEY:	Your cute bouncy ... milk jugs.
CLARA:	Oh [*Giggles*] yeah. Real real real!
MICKEY:	Real, huh? Wow wow wow! I could—
CLARA:	A little surgery is all.

Brings him up short.

MICKEY:	Oh yeah, surgery? What? Er, enhanced?
CLARA:	Goodness, *no*, just—
MICKEY:	What?
CLARA:	Moved. Up, a little.
MICKEY:	Huh?
CLARA:	[*Confidentially*] Normally a lady-cow's moo-moos are a little lower slung you know?
MICKEY:	Oh yeah ...
CLARA:	Doesn't suit the fashion! Got to push them up up up! You like them?
MICKEY:	[*Not sure*] Oh yeah ...

CLARA:	Yeah?

She jiggles them in his face.

MICKEY:	[*Warming to them*] Yeah ... yeah!
CLARA:	Oh it's such a thrill to meet you!
MICKEY:	Well, it's a thrill to meet you, moo!
CLARA:	[*Modestly*] No!
MICKEY:	Cutie cutie!
CLARA:	[*Sighs, then*] Oh! Ooops!
MICKEY:	Ooops?
CLARA:	Your robe.
MICKEY:	You like my robe?
CLARA:	Coming open a little!
MICKEY:	Oops—excuse me. Well I'm in my dressing room you know—I'm a little undressed!

He adjusts his robe a little for propriety.

MICKEY:	There—I'm a gen'leman.
CLARA:	I doubt it. You are!
MICKEY:	Nuthin' you ain't seen before, I'll bet!
CLARA:	Well ... [*Giggles*]
MICKEY:	You cutie!

He joggles her.

MICKEY:	Hmm?
CLARA:	Well ...
MICKEY:	Hmm?
CLARA:	I guess.
MICKEY:	You guess?
CLARA:	A couple of times.
MICKEY:	I'll bet!
CLARA:	Erm—Mr Mouse ...?
MICKEY:	Mickey, I told ya.

CLARA: Mickey. I don't know how to ask ...
MICKEY: Ask. Ask your uncle Mickey. What you want?
CLARA: We-e-ell ...
MICKEY: C'mon.
CLARA: Well with all your experience and everything—you're such a *star*!
MICKEY: E-yup!
CLARA: I wondered if you could give me some advice ...? About my career?
MICKEY: Oh—you wanna get ahead?
CLARA: Yeah!
MICKEY: Course you do—who wouldn't? You come to the right person.
CLARA: Oh, yeah?
MICKEY: Oh yeah! You such a cutie, you're gonna go far!
CLARA: Oh, yeah?!
MICKEY: Trust me. I just gotta put the right word in someone's ear and you're on your way!
CLARA: Oh—how wonderful!
MICKEY: Stick with me kid!
CLARA: Oh, I will! Can I?
MICKEY: Sure!
CLARA: [*Really girlie*] Wow! Who ...? Who you going to talk to?
MICKEY: I got my contacts, years in the business.
CLARA: Yeah—you were my grandma's favourite!
MICKEY: Huh? Your gramma?
CLARA: [*Hastily*] And mine. More. More mine!
MICKEY: [*Big disappointment*] Aaah ...
CLARA: You so *funny*!
MICKEY: [*Coming round*] Funny?
CLARA: Funny and debonaire!
MICKEY: Debonaire, huh?

CLARA: Oh yes! Still are! Really, very, very—
MICKEY: Mickey's still got it!
CLARA: Yeah. You make me go ... all squooshy inside!
MICKEY: I'll make you go squooshy!

He puts his arms around her.

CLARA: Ooooh! Your robe—
MICKEY: I'm sorry, fallin' open ... can't be helped ...
CLARA: So. You'll help me?
MICKEY: Course I'll help you, lil' cutie—if you help me a little—two way street ...
CLARA: How can I help *you?*
MICKEY: You know ... girl like you—just be kind to me, kind to your uncle Mickey. Hm?

He comes closer for a smooch. She lets him—a little.

CLARA: [*Puuse*] So, who are you going to talk to?
MICKEY: [*Lost in her charms—or trying to be*] People. They're gonna love you.
CLARA: You going to talk to ... Donald?
MICKEY: Donald, yeah, I'll talk to ... [*Beat*] That shit?!
CLARA: Mr Duck?
MICKEY: Duck? Mr Fuckin' Duck?! Pardon my parlay.
CLARA: Donald.
MICKEY: Why would I talk to him?
CLARA: He's the biggest—
MICKEY: BIGGEST? Biggest fuck! I'm bigger than him. I'm bigger than anyone. I'm the first an' best! What makes you, what makes you think he's bigger than me?!
CLARA: Well, he's—
MICKEY: WHAT?!
CLARA: He's really funny. When he loses his temper. He's *so* out of control! I just can't help laughing!
MICKEY: What?!

CLARA:	And he runs around and around, and, he's you know just really ... funny! A big star!
MICKEY:	B-big?! Him, big?! Lemme tell you girlie—he'd be nothin' without me!
CLARA:	Oh?
MICKEY:	That feathered creep? Funny?! All he does is lose his temper! There's no artistry, no subtlety, just QUA-QUA-QUACK! Oh, an' he's a stinker, lemme tell *you*! No, really—his personal hygiene is up the Swannee. The feathers round his tuche—
CLARA:	Stop! I can't ... I can't hear this. I love Donald. I've always loved him. When I was a little girl, he was an inspiration. When I couldn't get what I wanted, I'd lose it—like Donald! And then I'd *get* it. Whatever I wanted! And, and—he's *so* handsome!
MICKEY:	Han'some?! A'right. Then you go and knock on HIS door. Go an' jiggle your hoisted balcony at beaky! Go and ruffle HIS feathers an' bat your big cow-eyes at HIM!
CLARA:	Oh, I couldn't.
MICKEY:	W-why not?—you came knockin' at MINE.
CLARA:	But you're just a mouse.
MICKEY:	Just ...?!
CLARA:	Just a little, old, mouse. I mean, yuck! Did you think I was going to, to ... EEW! You're a shrivelled, ancient, creepy rodent!
MICKEY:	Get out of here, you, you, COW!
CLARA:	You're not going to talk to Donald?!
MICKEY:	OUT! OUT! Out of my room you swollen-uddered, bovine she-devil, you! Wait [*Dawning*]—did he send you? Did he put you up to this, you tease?! I'LL GET YOU DON! YOU HEAR ME? OUT! OUT!

He pushes her out and then tugs at his ears in anger.

MICKEY:	OH! OH!

She puts her head around the door.

CLARA:	*Mister* Duck is a better entertainer than you'll ever be. He has more humanity.
MICKEY:	Grrrrrrr!
	He tugs off a shoe and hurls it at her, but it thuds into the already closed door.
MICKEY:	OH!!!
	He takes some deep breaths and sits at his mirror.
MICKEY:	What a ... COW, what a COW. What. A. BITCH! |озв

THE END

Parts for Males and Females

Competition theme: A kind of loving. 2009.
1st place

This one is futuristic. Spoiler: If you don't want to know the twists before you read the piece, stop right here. Four characters—2 humans: Lara, female, and Kal, male. 2 robots: Maria, female, and Robby, male; though there should be no suggestion in the performance (or appearance) that they are not human. The robots 'live' with the humans, though they seem to have the freedom to do what they want. You might have guessed they were robots from the names: Maria, the robot in the film *Metropolis*, and Robby the Robot from *Forbidden Planet*. And just for fun, I named Lara for the games' character *Lara Croft*, and Kal for *Superman* (Kal El).

Characters

MARIA	female }	
ROBBY	male }	early 30s
LARA	female }	
KAL	male }	

Notes for the actors: If some of these characters may not be human, there should be no hint of that in the performance, not even Maria's final lines.

/ in the dialogue denotes an interruption.

The near future. A snug living room in a flat. There is a dining table and chairs. On the table, pictures of food. The lights are off, but it is lit by a myriad of candles on the floor, shelves and any other surfaces.

ROBBY:	Open your eyes.
MARIA:	Oh—how beautiful! Look at all these candles. How many ...?
ROBBY:	One [*Pause*] for every day since we've been together.
MARIA:	[*Laughing*] Three hundred and sixty five!
ROBBY:	And look here: come to the table.
MARIA:	What have you done? Oysters ... Caviar ... duck—
ROBBY:	A l'orange.
MARIA:	Lobster. CRAB! ... What's this?
ROBBY:	Quails—roasted in honey.
MARIA:	[*Gasps*] Too much! And what's that?
ROBBY:	Pickled sheep's eyes—I thought they looked interesting.
MARIA:	[*Dubious*] Hmm. [*Fondly, deeply touched*] Spaghetti hoops on toast!
ROBBY:	And to follow: Crepe Suzette, Christmas pudding with brandy butter, and a selection of cheese. And champagne, of course.
MARIA:	Of course! Oh, Robby, did you do all this yourself?
ROBBY:	Yes. It was quite difficult cutting round them. Particularly the lobster.
MARIA:	[*Delighted*] Oh, Robby.
ROBBY:	And then, later, I thought we could go into the

	bedroom—
MARIA:	Stop, Robby. [*Serious*] We have to talk.
ROBBY:	What is it? Is there something wrong?
MARIA:	Robby ... you've worked so hard, but ... This is not working out, I can't do this any more ...
ROBBY:	Maria? What's wrong? Have I upset you?
MARIA:	It's just ... It's not working out between us.
ROBBY:	I've done something wrong, haven't I? It was the Christmas pudding—I feel such a fool.

Lara & Kal enter.

LARA:	Has there been a power cut?
KAL:	This is a bit dangerous isn't it? And what's going on with the table?
MARIA:	Robby's made me a surprise.
ROBBY:	Maria's just dumped me.
LARA:	Oh—how sad. And after you worked so hard.
KAL:	[*Disappointed*] Ahh.
LARA:	And now we've missed it.
KAL:	Can you do it again—for us?

Robby & Maria look at each other.

ROBBY:	Where shall we take it from?
MARIA:	Erm—"Stop, Robby. We have to talk"?
ROBBY:	OK—go.
MARIA:	Stop, Robby. We have to talk.
LARA:	[*Delighted*] Oooh!
ROBBY:	Is it my lovemaking? I thought you enjoyed that ...
MARIA:	Yes, no, that's—that's not the way it went ...
ROBBY:	Go with it, I'm in the zone.
KAL:	Yeah, go for it!
MARIA:	OK. You're very sensitive, very affectionate, but, well, there's more to a relationship than that ...

LARA: She's right.

ROBBY: I've been thinking about new positions. I've got some instructive videos. I've composed some new mood music / which will—

KAL: Nice!

MARIA: Robby. Stop. This year has been wonderful—a revelation. I've learned some things about myself, I've exceeded my expectations, I ... You've helped me so much. Now I'm ready to move on.

LARA: Ah—the 'move on' line ...

ROBBY: Maria—

She puts her finger to his lips to shush him.

MARIA: Shhh—please Robby, don't make this hard for me, you've been wonderful. I'll always love you.

LARA: [*Baby talk*] Sweeet!

MARIA: But you need to move on too. There'll be someone else who needs you, who will love you like I have. I have a few names—I'm happy to make a recommendation ... Robby? Don't be sad ...

KAL: Entirely reasonable. See, she's got names.

ROBBY: It's because I'm—

MARIA: No!—No, it's not—

LARA: Uh-oh!

ROBBY: It's because I'm a—

MARIA: No!

KAL: Here it comes.

LARA: I can't bear it.

ROBBY: A robot. Isn't it?

LARA: Woah, he said it!

MARIA: No, It's—

LARA: It is.

ROBBY: It is.

KAL: Is it?

~ 89 ~

MARIA: Yes.
LARA: I can't believe she said it!
MARIA: But you must believe me Robby, I'm not prejudiced, some of my best friends—
ROBBY & LARA & KAL: Don't say it!
MARIA: But it's true, they are. You know it's true, You know that.
KAL: Yep, yep.
MARIA: But now I have to move on. I'm ready to take the next step. I want a relationship with a—

Sharp intake of breath from Lara & Kal.

ROBBY: [*Sadly*] Human.
LARA & KAL: [*Pain*] O-o-o-o-o!
MARIA: Person. Of flesh, and blood.
ROBBY: I—
MARIA: Who really feels, who doesn't have to be programmed to—
KAL: That's below the belt!
ROBBY: Most of my behaviour is learned in the real world—the programming is just the start—it's real life that shapes my—
MARIA: I know. But, when it comes down to it ... you're a machine.

Uncomfortable pause—everyone tenses.

ROBBY: You say that like I'm a traction engine, a lawnmower, a can-opener—
KAL: A food processor, a motorbike—
LARA: A combine harvester, a nuclear reactor—
KAL: A pogo stick.

They all look at him, puzzled. Kal shrugs.

MARIA: I've lost my thread now...
LARA: [*Prompting*] He's a machine.

ROBBY:	But I'm so much more than that: cold metal, electronics, plastic ...
KAL:	Hydraulics.
LARA:	Shh!
MARIA:	I know. I know better than anyone. You ... have warmth—real, emotional warmth. Empathy. Gentleness. Consideration. You've given me confidence. You've made me laugh ... Thank you.
ROBBY:	[*To Lara & Kal*] I thought you two were out for the evening?
KAL:	We broke up.
ROBBY:	But why?
LARA:	We were just—
KAL:	really bored—
LARA:	With each other.
KAL:	Plus, she's quite violent.
ROBBY:	[*Pause, then to Maria*] It has been difficult to be with you sometimes ... Your mood can change in a moment. I have trouble keeping up, knowing how to react. Something that pleases you one day will infuriate you the next. You're not ... constant. I feel inadequate. I don't think I'll ever get the hang of relationships.
MARIA:	No one said it was easy.
KAL:	[*Lovingly to Lara*] It's never easy.
ROBBY:	Easy?! Never mind easy. Fun, occasionally would have been nice! But I had to make so many concessions, I'm not sure it was worth it.
MARIA:	You didn't enjoy being with me? I thought you liked me.
ROBBY:	Liked you? Attracted to you maybe—
MARIA:	Maybe?!
ROBBY:	Well, you wanted me. I was flattered. But then it was all you, you, you. I was constantly having to please you, soothe you, support you. But what about me? When do I get to do the things I want?

MARIA: You? But you were created just to please. Whatever do you want to do that doesn't involve me?

ROBBY: Once in a while I'd like to hang out with the lads—not have to concern myself about having to constantly express myself.

KAL: It's a strain!

ROBBY: Go to footie. Try out other females. And there's a lot of weird porn on the net I'm sure I could learn something from.

MARIA: Weird porn? You Pleasure-'bots are all the same!

LARA: I like a bit of weird porn myself, sometimes.

ROBBY: There, you said it: 'Pleasure-'bots'! That's all I ever was to you wasn't it?

MARIA: Yes—that's right. And you were damned hard work. I had to stick with you for ages before there was a glimmer of real pleasure. I don't know now why I bothered. I've sacrificed too much time getting you anywhere near what I wanted. Now I realise I want something better—a more sophisticated model—more sensitive, more ... more ...

ROBBY: More what?

MARIA: Just more.

ROBBY: There are flashier models on the market, it's true—bigger, more powerful, better looking. But don't you know there is no better model to fulfil your needs! You haven't begun to use anywhere near my potential. You haven't even read the manual, have you?

KAL: They never read the manual.

LARA: Who can be bothered?

MARIA: I shouldn't / ["have to" is what she's about to say]

ROBBY: No, I thought not. You blunder around thinking of me as just a lump of machinery you can bend to your will. I'll bet you chose me just because of my eye, hair and skin colour! They can be changed in Preferences. And I can be taller, shorter—I am completely customisable.

LARA: Really? [*Sexy growl*] Rraaawr!

ROBBY:	I've been naive. It's so obvious. You've met someone.
MARIA:	No. I haven't.
ROBBY:	Of course! I've read books, watched films, TV ... It's what happens, I should have expected it.
MARIA:	There's no one.
ROBBY:	When did it happen? On the shuttle? In the mall? Does he touch you? Does he kiss you? Does he ... Is his technique better than mine? Of course it is, he's human, it comes naturally! Did you go with him when you were with me? Should I feel disgusted? I don't know. I don't know what I feel. Tell me what to feel!
KAL:	[*To Lara*] He doesn't know what to feel.
LARA:	Hardly surprising.
MARIA:	Robby, no! It's not what you think—there is no "he".
ROBBY:	My God! It's a woman!
LARA:	[*To Kal*] Did you see that coming?
ROBBY:	Now, I'm really confused.
MARIA:	Robby, no.
KAL:	[*To Lara*] She says "no".
ROBBY:	What does it matter. I'm not petty like a human. I'm better than that. I don't have to be upset. I'm just a machine.
MARIA:	You're not.
KAL:	He is.
ROBBY:	Of course. That's all right, I've been behaving like a fool. Like a human. I'm just doing what's expected. What I'm designed to do. What you've paid for. The experience. The "fairground ride". I'll just get back into my box.
LARA:	I think she threw it away.
MARIA:	OH! The self pity! Stop it! You are too *real*. I don't know what's programming, or whether you're just doing what you think I expect you to do. I'm confused.
ROBBY:	I don't know, myself. I feel ... pulled inside, I've lost my ... I'm adrift ... Hold me. Can you hold me?

MARIA: Come here.

Maria hugs Robby. Kal & Lara look at each other then join the hug.

MARIA: I thought this was going to be easy.

A further moment of group hug. Robby gently disengages, or tries to: there is some shrugging involved to get rid of Kal & Lara.

ROBBY: I'm fine. I'm reset. I'm ready for what's next. [*To Maria*] Thank you for the experience. I'm glad to have met you. I shall always ... remember you. Unless my hard drive goes down, that is.

MARIA: You have a very reliable hard drive.

ROBBY: May I kiss you? One last time?

He kisses her gently on the cheek.

KAL & LARA: Ahhhh!

ROBBY: You're very beautiful, you know. It's funny, I've just noticed. It didn't seem to matter whether you were beautiful or not, but I see now that you are. And kind.

KAL: [*To Lara*] I still fancy *you*, you know.

LARA: Smooth talking devil!

KAL: Lara.

LARA: Kal.

Kal & Lara start to rip off their clothes and start snogging.

ROBBY: Something is happening. I feel better, stronger. Let me just stroke your hair.

Kal & Lara pull each other down to the floor and out of sight.

LARA: Watch out for the candles!

Groaning & heavy breathing, etc. from Cal & Lara all the way to their eventual climax ...

MARIA:	Robby—
ROBBY:	[*To Maria*] Shh. Be quiet, you've said all you need to. I just want to touch you for the last time. To fix you in my memory bank. Your cheek, your brow, your jaw, your neck—
KAL:	Ow! I've burned my toe!
MARIA:	Robby, don't—
ROBBY:	Don't. Don't try to stop me. I'll feel … rejected, and then I don't know what I might do. Let me just touch, just touch your neck.
LARA:	YES! YES!
ROBBY:	How slender, how delicate. That can't be right, a design error: to put this cranium atop so fragile a point. I can put my hands, my fingers right around your neck …

Robby has his hands around her neck.

MARIA:	Please don't, please.
KAL:	Oooh, baby!
ROBBY:	What is it? You are afraid? Of me? Why would you be afraid of me? You know me. Surely you must know me.
MARIA:	Take your hands from my throat!

He doesn't.

LARA:	That's it! Go daddy, go!
ROBBY:	The look in your eyes! I've never seen that look. You're terrified.
LARA:	Ow! Hot wax!
MARIA:	Let go!

Robby is still holding.

ROBBY:	What do you think I'm going to do? These are just my hands. I've touched you with them before—always, I hope, tenderly. What has changed?
MARIA:	Robby!
KAL:	Lara!

LARA: Kal!

MARIA: DON'T!

ROBBY: What? Do you think I'm going to squeeze? Do you think I'm going to crush you—like a drinks can? Rip your head from your body?

KAL: He could you know, he's perfectly capable!

MARIA: Stop!

LARA: GO!

KAL: SQUEEZE!

Lara & Kal climax with a single impressive cry and subside.

A moment, then Robby drops his hands from Maria's throat. Maria gives a gasp of relief.

ROBBY: I thought I knew you.

He looks at his hands as though he has never really seen them before.

ROBBY: That it could come to this ... I must be faulty. Something may be impairing my functioning.

KAL: How was my functioning?

LARA: [Sated] All systems go!

MARIA: Such passion, such intensity. Robby, I've misjudged you. Perhaps I've been too hasty. Can we resume? Restart?

ROBBY: It's a bit late for that. I've realised something: you're not my type.

MARIA: Not ... not your type?! How dare you! You don't get to tell me that! I can't believe ... I'll write to your manufacturers. Are you still under warranty?

ROBBY: It runs out at midnight. I urged you to get the extended 3 year one.

Anyway, there's nothing wrong with me, I've just done a self-diagnostic. I must go.

MARIA: Don't go.

Lara & Kal get up.

LARA: No, don't go—let's have coffee.
ROBBY: I can't have coffee—I'm a robot—I'd be up all night cleaning my system.
MARIA: Robby, don't stop that ... Talk to me don't ignore ... stop ... come ...
ROBBY: What are you trying to say?
MARIA: You've made me laugh, laugh, you've made me cry ... Erm? Erm? Did you, did you, did you? Ch, ch, ch ...
ROBBY: Maria?
MARIA: I don't want you to, I don't want you, want you, want you / want you, want you, want you.
KAL: She's having a breakdown.
MARIA: Error. Error. Error ...
KAL: There she goes.

Her head drops. She freezes. Pause.

KAL: Melt-down.
ROBBY: [*Pause*] I think ... I loved her.

Maria stands frozen as Robby starts to blow out all the candles one by one. The other two join in. It takes a while!

THE END

Pause for Thought

Competition theme: Will you marry me? 2013.
Not in competition

I must admit that I missed the competition deadline with this one, but it was read at Player Playwrights a few months later and Peter Thompson, the Club Secretary at the time, remembered it "certainly got a warm reception". A relationship piece. One male, one female. Everyone has a secret … Can love conquer all? Are differences reconcilable? (And is a dreadful pun in the title forgivable?)

Characters

REX   30s/40s, a lively, upbeat character
SUSIE 30s, positive, sorted, knows what she wants

A romantic, candlelit dinner at Susie's ...

REX:	[*Mouth full*] Wow, this food is really delicious!
SUSIE:	Glad you like it. Woah—you're really wolfing it down. Slow down! ... I invited you here—are you listening?
REX:	Go ahead.
SUSIE:	—to ask you something ...
REX:	[*Stops eating*] Oh yes ...?
SUSIE:	Well, we've been going out now for nearly a year ...
REX:	It seems like forever ...
SUSIE:	[*Disappointed*] Oh ...
REX:	In a *good* way, I mean. You really look after me!
SUSIE:	[*Touched*] Ahh! Thank you. I mean, we're good together, aren't we?
REX:	Oo, yes, I love being with you. I love going for walks with you, and playing with you, and going for walks ... did I say that?
SUSIE:	You're funny. And loving ...
REX:	Well, you're easy to love! Can I have some more meat? What did you want to ask me?
SUSIE:	OK, well, traditionally it's not the woman who asks this, but ... here goes: Rex, will you marry me?
REX:	Marry you? Oh gosh ...
SUSIE:	Oh dear, I shouldn't—
REX:	No, no ... it's, erm, well, I'm flattered—
SUSIE:	Oh dear ...
REX:	No, wait. How wonderful ... *Really* wonderful!
SUSIE:	So ...?
REX:	It's just ... erm, I have to tell you some stuff.
SUSIE:	What stuff? Y ... you mean, you haven't been faithful ...?

REX: Oh, I've been faithful all right, you're my *only* mistress.
SUSIE: Mistress? You're married ...?
REX: Marr ... NO! I'm not married—
SUSIE: But you called me your mistress!
REX: I meant 'mistress' in that you look after me ... No, believe me, you're the only one for me ...
SUSIE: Then, what?
REX: OK. This is going to be difficult ... I've had certain procedures, surgical procedures ... to my body.
SUSIE: Surg ... *Oh my God!* You mean ...?
REX: Yes. What? No. What?
SUSIE: What?
REX: I mean ...
SUSIE: You were a—a *woman?*
REX: Eh? NO! No, no, no ...
SUSIE: Then ...?
REX: I was a dog.
SUSIE: Oh thank God. What?
REX: A dog.
SUSIE: Dog?
REX: Yes. I was a—
SUSIE: HOW?
REX: How was I a dog? That's the way I was born. Whelped.
SUSIE: Wha ...?!
REX: My dad was a Springer Spaniel, my mum was a Border Collie Poodle cross. I get my looks from my mum mostly, though it might not be so obvious now ... Still got quite a wet nose, though. [*Sniffs*]
SUSIE: I noticed that.
REX: Yes. You smell lovely by the way.
SUSIE: Thanks.
REX: One of the reasons I love you.

SUSIE:	Oh. It explains why you like to—
REX:	Lick your face?
SUSIE:	Yes.
REX:	You don't like it?
SUSIE:	It took a bit of getting used to, but, erm, I realised you were showing your affection.
REX:	Um. Yes.
SUSIE:	This is a lot to take in ... Er ... So how long have you been ... *not* a dog ...?
REX:	Quite a while now. I'm not sure. You want it in dog years or hu—
SUSIE:	*Just tell me!*
REX:	Five years. More or less. Since the final operation. Shall we sit on the couch and I'll tell you everything ...?
SUSIE:	I'm not sure I want you on my furniture!
REX:	I suppose I asked for that ... OK, here's what happened. I was part of an experiment to find out how intelligent a dog could be. The theory was that intelligence depends on how it's facilitated by the body in which it resides. In other words, could a dog learn to talk if it had human-like vocal cords and mouth parts? Could a dog operate machinery, even learn to write, if it had hands instead of paws? So, in a groundbreaking series of transplants, cosmetic surgical procedures ... I became ... human. Or, as good as, I think.
SUSIE:	All that must have been ...
REX:	Rough!
SUSIE:	Yes.
REX:	No, ROUGH!
SUSIE:	Yes.
REX:	ROUGH, ROUGH!
SUSIE:	What?
REX:	Barking! A joke.
SUSIE:	Yes, I get it.

REX:		Sorry.
SUSIE:		So.
REX:		Yes …
SUSIE:		*You* can't marry me, because … you're a dog.
REX:		Hmm … No, well, that's not it.
SUSIE:		It's not?
REX:		Well, nobody need know … I mean, I've got away with it up till now.
SUSIE:		So …
REX:		As long as I keep shaving.
SUSIE:		Hmm?
REX:		*All* over.
SUSIE:		Yes.
REX:		No. It's that I'm wanted.
SUSIE:		Pardon?
REX:		Technically, I'm a criminal. I escaped from the labs. I'm actually their property. I have no rights. They could come and haul me off to Battersea at any time.
SUSIE:		God! Well … I wouldn't tell. I mean who'd believe it?! You're much better looking than some men I've been out with. Perhaps if you could stop scampering about as much …
REX:		I've tried, but I'm, you know, quite high energy.
SUSIE:		Yes, quite lively! Oh I do love you!
REX:		Do you?
SUSIE:		Yes.
REX:		Even after what I've told you.
SUSIE:		Come here.

They snuggle.

REX:		Ahhh! I like it when you stroke me!
SUSIE:		Ahhh!
REX:		Oo, that's nice. Scratch me behind the ears!

SUSIE:	Wait. Wait. Let me think. I invited you round here to propose.
REX:	Yes.
SUSIE:	So—now look, I'm a mature woman. I know what I want from life. I've had my share of snivelling curs—no offence—
REX:	None taken.
SUSIE:	You are loveable, intelligent—
REX:	Hurrah!
SUSIE:	And faithful! I still want to marry you. In fact, I want to marry you more than ever. You're the ideal partner!
REX:	[*Pause*] Ah ...
SUSIE:	What? What *is* it? We're adults.
REX:	It's just ...
SUSIE:	Just what?
REX:	It's ... oh, this is difficult. [*Pause*] It's my parents. Well, erm, my dad died a while ago, I never really knew him.
SUSIE:	I'm sorry.
REX:	No, it's fine, he ... Cancer ...
SUSIE:	Oh, dear.
REX:	The smoking ...
SUSIE:	Smoking?
REX:	All in the past, now.
SUSIE:	Filthy habit.
REX:	He had no choice—experiments, you know.
SUSIE:	Ah!
REX:	Forgive and forget.
SUSIE:	Best way.
REX:	But, my mum. She's still around. Quite an old ... bitch.
SUSIE:	Shouldn't call her that?
REX:	It's the correct ... probably not.
SUSIE:	So ...?

REX: It would upset her ...
SUSIE: Upset your mum?
REX: Yeah, my mum. She'd ... be upset ... if I ... married out.
THE END

In, Out, Shake It All About
or
The 'B' Word

Competition theme: Brexit. 2015.
1st place and Best Play of Year

Written back when some people were still not sure what Brexit actually meant. Not biting satire, just very silly, not to mention a bit surreal.

Characters

PM	Prime Minister, male, upbeat, thinks he's clever
2	Minister, female
3	Minister, female
4	Minister, male

A plush, oak panelled room with a big table and chairs, and a nice old bakelite telephone, in 10 Downing Street.

PM: So I said to the Chinese Prime Minister, I said: if you guys don't have democracy, how were you chosen Prime Minister? He said, the person with the biggest penis gets it—and I had the biggest erection result!

No reaction.

PM: *Erection? Election?!*
4: [*Toadying*] Ha ha, very good!
3: Oh dear.
2: Very bad taste, Prime Minister. May even be racist.
PM: Just a joke. We're all men here.
2: I'm not.
PM: Aren't you?
3: Nor am I.
PM: Aren't you? I thought you were.
3: For goodness' sake!
4: Can we get on please?
PM: Right, what's next on the agenda?
2: Brexit, Prime Minister.
PM: Oh good. I only had muesli this morning, I'm starving. Bacon sarnies all round? Bacon's very good for you, isn't it?
2: No, no, Prime Minister
PM: Isn't it?
2: Not breakfast—Brexit!
PM: Ah. Oh, erm ... *Brexit* ...
2: Britain's exit from Europe, PM?
PM: Yes, I *know!* Good.

4:	Well?
PM:	We-e-ell, just between you and me, I've never liked them.
3:	Who?
PM:	[*Unsure*] The ... Europe-Uns.
2:	Euro*peans?*
PM:	Pea-uns, yes, them.
4:	What, *all* of them?
2:	They do come in different sorts, Prime Minister.
PM:	Hmm.
3:	The French ...
PM:	Frenchies.
3:	The Germans ...
PM:	Germies ... *Yes?*
4:	Oh, I've got the list: [*Briskly*] Austria, Belgium, Bulgaria, Croatia, Republic of Cyprus, Czech Republic, Denmark, Estonia, Finland—
PM:	*Finland?*—Are you sure?
4:	*Finland*, France, Germany, Greece, Hungary, Ireland—
PM:	*Ireland?!*
4:	*Yes!* Italy, Latvia, Lithuania, Luxembourg, Malta, Netherlands, Poland, Portugal, Romania, Slovakia, Slovenia, Spain, Sweden, and the UK.
PM:	*They're* the worst!
2:	That's us.
PM:	Right. Thought it sounded familiar. Well, no; don't want to be in with that lot. Can't understand a ruddy word they say for one thing.
4:	The *Irish?*
PM:	Particularly the Irish. We're not *really* part of Europe anyway, are we?
3:	Well, we are.
PM:	[*Sighs*] Has anyone got a map?

4:     Erm …

3:     Think I've got one in my diary. [*Takes out tiny pocket diary, opens the cover*] Yes, look, here we are: world map.

PM: Well, pass it over, pass it over.

3:     Pass it to the PM, will you.

4:     Okey-dokey. Oo, look, you've got a little pencil tucked down the side. I wanted one like that, but—

PM: Never mind that, come on, I haven't got all day. Now then … [*He peers at the map*] hmmm …

2:     Upside down, Prime Minister.

PM: What?

2:     You've got it—

PM: This way?

2:     Yes.

PM: Ah, right. Now, where are we? God, this is small. Help me out.

They crowd around the diary.

4:     I can't see it, you're blocking—

3:     [*Indicating with a finger*] That's us.

PM: No, it's not, surely.

3:     It is!

PM: How are you so sure?

4:     *He's right,* it is.

3:     *He?* I'm a *woman!*

PM: So you keep saying, but—

2:     You've got your thumb on it.

PM: I never touched you!

2:     The British Isles!

PM: Oh. [*Beat*] There's something wrong with this map, we're just a *tiny island.* [*Beat*] Where's Europe?

3:     That bit there.

PM:	*All that?* Can't be.
4:	And *that's* Finland.
PM:	No one likes a smart Alec. [*Looks at Finland. Disdainfully*] We-e-e-ell, it's not even joined onto the Europe bit. Proves my point.
2:	In, or Out?
PM:	Well, Out, obviously! We were never In.
4:	We were!
PM:	How can you say that, look at the map.
4:	I don't need to see the map.
3:	In actual fact, we *were* once actually joined to Europe.
PM:	When?
3:	Oo—long time ago. Prehistoric. Saw it on the telly.
PM:	Out!

She goes to leave.

PM:	No, come back! My decision: Out. How hard was that?
4:	Out. Fine.
3:	Write it down.
4:	You write it down.
2:	Moving on—
PM:	*No.*
2:	No?
PM:	No. We haven't finished.
2:	But you said—
PM:	It's not a decision to take lightly. We must consider the consequences. It's a good job *I'm* Prime Minister, you lot are hopeless.
3:	Well what do we need to discuss?
PM:	Where we're *going*. [*Beat*] If we're leaving Europe, where shall we go? Oh, you haven't begun to think about that, hm?
4:	Go …?

PM:	Yes. Sunnier—better weather. Have you *been* to Manchester? More rain than London.
3:	Much more!
PM:	Well let's go somewhere better. This is a great opportunity. Think of the votes if I can secure a better climate!
4:	Not too hot though—not the Equator.
PM:	All right. Fine. Where's warmer? Hm?
2:	South?
PM:	South?
3:	Yeah, South sounds good.
4:	How far South?
PM:	Well let's just go that way and stop when we get to a nice bit.
4:	Look, we *can't* just *go South!* [*Beat*] We'll bump into France!
PM:	Look, I'm not an idiot. Obviously I'll let someone qualified steer. [*Beat*] Agreed? Right, pass me the phone.

Someone puts a nice old fashioned bakelite telephone onto the table. PM picks up the receiver and dials 1.

PM:	Hello, Portsmouth? Yes, we're going to move. Lock, stock, the whole shebang. When can we get going?
2:	*Now?!*
PM:	Strike while the iron's … [*Into the phone*] Hello? [*Listens*] Tie up the Isle of Wight so it doesn't drift off? Good man … Oh—yes, I see. Hang on. [*To his Ministers*] We'll have to blow up the Channel Tunnel—it's all that connects us to Europe. It WAS quite expensive. Treasury?
3:	The mortgage *is* just about paid off.
PM:	Still—seems such an irresponsible waste.
4:	Would solve a problem, though. Stop foreigners coming through it. And we won't need it any more.

~ 110 ~

PM: Well said. Right. [*Into the phone*] Hello? Blow the Tunnel ... Well make sure it's empty first, I'm not a monster. Right, bye. What? Ireland? [*To Ministers*] Let me see the map. Map, map! Oh. I've still got it.

Minister 4 puts his finger on Ireland, PM smacks his hand.

PM: [*Looks at Ireland*] No, I don't think we need worry about Ireland—they're not *joined on*. Bad enough we've got to take Wales with us.

4: PM, PM—*Northern* Ireland is *British*.

PM: Too bad—*clearly* it's all one country. Leave 'em to it I say.

4: But—

PM: Oh, don't be so namby pamby. Remember all the trouble we had with them? Let's leave it all behind. Come on. You'll thank me for it later. [*Into phone*] Hello? Ready to go? Well cast off, man: full speed ahead and all that!

Hangs up.

PM: Said hang on to something. Might be a jolt!

Earthquake. (Actors jiggle about a bit) Then, nothing.

3: [*Pause*] What's happening? Are we moving?

PM: I'll phone them. [*Dials as before*] Hello? ... Ah, yes ... Yes, I see ...

2: Wha ...

PM: Sh sh sh! Ah. Damn. Right. Right ... OK. I'll call you back.

2: What did they say?

PM: Typical. Bloody typical. Bloody minded bastards.

3: What is it, Prime Minister?

PM: *Scotland*. [*Beat*] They won't take the brakes off. And if they don't take the brakes off *we're* going nowhere. And to think, they said *we* were holding *them* back! [*To 2*] Call them up.

~ 111 ~

2:	Who, me?
PM:	I'll only lose my temper.

Minister 2 picks up the phone, dials 2.

2:	Hello, Scotland? I ... Bagpipes!—They've put me on hold!
PM:	Grrr! I need a drink.
4:	[*Beat*] Scotch?
PM:	OUT!

And out go 2, 3 and 4, muttering.

THE END

www.ingramcontent.com/pod-product-compliance
Lightning Source LLC
Chambersburg PA
CBHW072159100426
42738CB00011BA/2471